MW00476721

THE TIME HAS COME

GER McDONNELL
HIS LIFE & HIS DEATH ON K2

To
Lynn
Best wishes
Jason O...

To Denise, Mam & Dad

THE TIME HAS COME

GER McDONNELL
HIS LIFE & HIS DEATH ON K2

DAMIEN O'BRIEN

The Collins Press

First published in 2012 by
The Collins Press
West Link Park
Doughcloyne
Wilton
Cork

© Damien O'Brien 2012

Damien O'Brien has asserted his moral right to be identified as the author of this work in accordance with the Copyright and Related Rights Act 2000.

All rights reserved.
The material in this publication is protected by copyright law. Except as may be permitted by law, no part of the material may be reproduced (including by storage in a retrieval system) or transmitted in any form or by any means, adapted, rented or lent without the written permission of the copyright owners. Applications for permissions should be addressed to the publisher.

British Library Cataloguing in Publication data
O'Brien, Damien.
The time has come : Ger McDonnell : his life & his death on K2.
1. McDonnell, Gerard, 1971-2008. 2. McDonnell, Gerard, 1971-2008—Death and burial. 3. Mountaineering expeditions—Pakistan—K2 (Mountain) 4. Mountaineering accidents—Pakistan—K2 (Mountain) 5. Mountaineers—Ireland—Death.
I. Title
796.5'22'092-dc23

ISBN-13: 9781848891432

Design and typesetting by Fairways Design
Typeset in Minion Pro
Printed in Italy by Printer Trento

Photos courtesy the McDonnell family archive unless otherwise credited.

Pages vi–vii: Climbing on the lower slopes of K2
(Courtesy Wilco van Rooijen)

CONTENTS

'The Mountain' by Máire Ní Shúilleabháin   vii

Author's Note   viii

Acknowledgements   viii

Who's Who   x

Foreword   xii

1. K2 Summit: Triumph and Tragedy   1

2. Arrival in Pakistan (and Build-up for Denali Climb)   14

3. The Trek to K2 Base Camp (and Ger's Early Years)   24

4. The Start of the K2 Ascent (and Denali Summit and Rescue) 44

5. Waiting on K2 (and From Denali to Everest)   58

6. New Arrivals on K2 (and Recalling the Everest Summit)   73

7. Further Delay on K2 (and Bringing Hurling to Everest)   86

8. Weather Despair on K2 (and Everest Homecoming
    and Intervening Trips)   97

9. Final Summit Meeting (and K2 2006 and
    the Decision to Return)   114

10. Storm at Camp 3 (and Injury at K2, 2006)   125

11. Beyond Endurance (and a Cup of Tea on Denali)   135

12. Full Story after K2 Summit: Drama at Home   152

13. Family Travels to Islamabad   159

14. Media versus the McDonnells: Home from Pakistan   171

15. Immediate Aftermath and Legacy   177

Index   190

THE MOUNTAIN

To dare to be different;
To have the courage, wisdom and clarity of
Purpose to meet the challenge;
To put enough trust in God, to climb the highest
Mountain he created;
To be close to the stars;
Yet not lose sight of earth and the valleys below;
To pause for a moment, in a vision of perfect peace;
To be a great leader, yet a humble hero,
To have a dream, to follow it to the end,
And despite all the hardships,
Make that dream come true;
That is truly living!

Máire Ní Shúilleabháin
Teacher of Ger's at Kilcornan National School

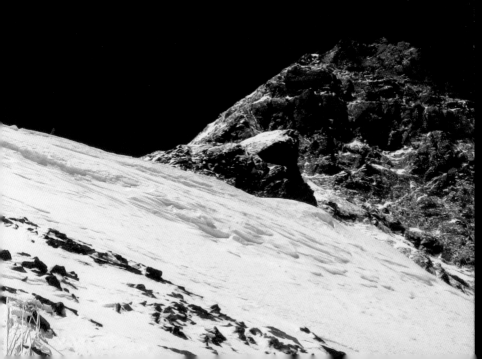

AUTHOR'S NOTE

In August 2008 Ger McDonnell fulfilled his ambition to reach the summit of the world's most dangerous mountain, K2.

While every chapter in this book deals with the K2 challenge and the preparations over many years, they also explore many other events, at different times in Ger's life. Hopefully the format succeeds in developing the story of how an ordinary, down-to-earth person from a small parish in County Limerick, through skill, determination and endurance, managed to conquer what remains the most fearsome of challenges and realise a long-held dream.

ACKNOWLEDGEMENTS

Write a book! I relished the initial idea of doing so; how hard could it be? Well, I never thought it would be so hard. This book contains mere snippets of the life that was Ger McDonnell's.

To Denise, my wife, for your patience in putting up with my being on the computer at all hours. Over the time it took me to complete this book I reopened a lot of memories for Denise of Ger – having books, pictures and paper cuttings of Ger scattered all over the place didn't help with her grieving. To my daughters Rebecca and Emma, I want to thank both of you for never stopping asking questions. I hope in the years to come both of you can look back over this book and realise how lucky you were to have an uncle like Ger.

To Gertie, Denis (RIP) and all the McDonnell family. Gertie, both you and Denis raised Ger and instilled in him the characteristics that made him the man he was. To J. J., Martha, Stephanie and Denise, your support was always noticed by Ger down through the years and he always loved you for that and never forgot.

To the friends and extended family of Ger's, Ger would always stay in touch. In carrying out research for this book I came into contact with some wonderful people who loved Ger and gladly shared their stories with me.

To Annie and Ger's friends in Alaska, Ger was having the time of his life in Alaska: it was his home away from home and I know he will never be forgotten there and we thank you for that.

To Ger's climbing community of friends, Pat Falvey, Clare O'Leary, Pemba Gyalje, Alan Arnette, Mark Sheen and all his Norit teammates just to name a few, I thank you for sharing in Ger's dreams and for your words of wisdom along the way.

To my own family, my mother Marie and father Ger for the kindness and support both of you always offered me, I thank you both. To my sister Karen and brother Patrick for being there to support me.

To my friend Amanda for being at hand whenever help was needed. To my secondary school English teacher Noel Malone, thank you for giving me the vision and encouragement to write as a student. That skill lay dormant for many years but thankfully woke up again.

On behalf of the McDonnell family, I want to thank everyone in the parish of Kilcornan and surrounding parishes for their unbelievable support at the time of Ger's death and continued support to this day. The family will never be able to repay your kindness.

To everyone who had an input into this book and who supported it.

The final and most important thank you has to go to Ger. I have never met such a remarkable man. Writing this book was made a lot easier by the fact that Ger himself wrote some of it. Thankfully Ger, you had the vision to log and make notes on most of your adventures.

You had the dream and you lived your life accordingly. Thank you for showing us the beauty of the world. Without you we would never have experienced it.

WHO'S WHO
(NAMES IN BOLD PLAY A MAJOR
PART ON K2 IN AUGUST 2008)

Norit K2 Dutch International Expedition 2008

Wilco – Wilco van Rooijen, Expedition Leader
Cas – Cas van de Gevel, Dutch climber, friend and climbing partner of Wilco since university
Ger – Gerard McDonnell, met Wilco on K2 in 2006
Pemba – Pemba Gyalje, Nepalese sherpa
Mark Sheen – Australian climber on Dutch Expedition
Roeland van Oss
Court Haegens
Jelle Staleman

Marco – Marco Confortola, Italian independent climber, professional mountain guide

Alberto Zerain – Basque independent climber

Dren Mandić – climber on Serbian K2 Vojvodina Expedition 2008
Shaheen Baig – lead guide/High-altitude Porter (HAP) with Serbian team

Cecilie – Cecilie Skog, leader of Norwegian K2 Expedition
Rolf – Rolf Bae, Cecilie's husband, climber on Norwegian Expedition
Lars – Lars Nessa, climber on Norwegian Expedition

Eric Meyer – anaesthestist, on American K2 International Expedition
Chris Klinke – member of American Expedition
Fredrik Strang – Swedish member of American Expedition
Chhiring Dorje – owner of Kathmandu-based guide service; sherpa on the American Expedition

Hugues – Hugues d'Aubarède, leader of Independent French Expedition
Karim Meherban – HAP working for French Expedition, climbing partner to Hugues
Jehan Baig – HAP working for French Expedition

Kim Jae-soo – leader of South Korean K2 Flying Jump Expedition
Go Mi-sun – female star climber with South Korean team

Jumik Bhote – sherpa with Korean Expedition
Tsering Bhote – sherpa with Korean Expedition, Jumik's brother
'Big' Pasang Bhote – sherpa with Korean Expedition, Jumik's cousin
'Little' Pasang Lama – sherpa with Korean Expedition, carried down the Bottleneck by Chhiring Dorje
Kim Hyo-gyeong – Korean climber found by Ger tangled in ropes
Park Kyeong-hyo – Korean climber found by Ger tangled in ropes
Hwang Dong-jin – Korean climber found by Ger tangled in ropes

FOREWORD

K2 is a beautiful mountain but remains one of the most difficult among the giants of the earth. Natural monuments are living according to natural laws. Often unknown to us, these natural beauties can be wild and hostile.

Man has always had a respect for and a special attraction to the contemplation of these monuments of nature. Others have felt so delighted that they decide to try climbing them, some for their own personal ambition, to explore human limitations, others for pure fun and uniqueness, others by blind and exclusive ego just to inflate their chest.

It happens, however, that when mountains suddenly become more manageable, fatalities can occur, sometimes due to human errors, coupled with bad luck. Then an exciting climb can be transformed into a large collective tragedy.

When someone dies they lose their voice to exactly what happened after the dust settles; often these true stories are in contradiction with those of other survivors or maybe some witnesses stay calm and silent.

K2 in 2008 had all these elements. There is more than one truth, and different types of heroes and leaders.

Certainly no one climbed the mountain to die, much less to escape life. But we have to learn a lot from each other, honestly, without finding an excuse. The memories of those who died on K2 in 2008 have to be remembered. Ger McDonnell went out of his way and spared no effort to help those who asked for assistance.

The Time Has Come tells a fantastic tale of true heroism and determination against the odds. It is not just about Ger's last few months while on K2 but is also the story of his life – a short one but one filled with excitement and adventure.

Simone Moro
January 2012

Climbing and ferrying loads on the lower slopes of K2.
(COURTESY WILCO VAN ROOIJEN)

CAMP FOUR

CAMP THREE

CAMP TWO

CAMP ONE

The Cesen route up K2 showing the
five camps. (Courtesy Nick Ryan)

BASE CAMP

1. K2 SUMMIT:
TRIUMPH AND TRAGEDY

It was just before 8 a.m. on 1 August 2008. The weather conditions were perfect for a summit attempt on K2 – little or no wind, light snow underfoot and sunshine. The pre-dawn temperature of minus 20 degrees celsius had been warmed by the sun reflecting on the snow to such an extent that some of the climbers opened their down suits, as they took a much-needed break while waiting to climb a steep, narrow gully of rock, ice and snow nicknamed the Bottleneck. Among the large group of experienced international climbers who had waited up to two months for this opportunity was Ger McDonnell, who was climbing with a Dutch expedition sponsored by the water purification multinational company, Norit, and led by Wilco van Rooijen.

Ger (left) and Wilco. (Courtesy Wilco Van Rooijen)

Wilco, 41, had spent almost a year putting the expedition together, raising sponsorship and supervising logistics. He was a driven character with a larger-than-life personality, but also a popular leader and a photogenic figurehead with blond curls and a winning smile. Ger, 37, had climbed with Wilco on K2 in 2006, and impressed him with his ability as a climber, his calmness and perseverance and his pleasant personality. Both Ger and Wilco had suffered near fatal accidents on K2 in the past, a bond which Wilco believed would motivate them in their determination to conquer the massive mountain this time around. Ger was one of three 'foreigners' selected for the eight-man Dutch expedition, the others being Pemba Gyalje,

The route to the summit of K2 from Camp 4. (Courtesy Nick Ryan)

the sherpa with whom Ger had climbed Mount Everest in 2003, and Australian climber Mark Sheen.

K2 is in the remote Karakoram range near the Himalayas on the border of China and Pakistan. It is the highest summit in a huge and remote mountain range that contains eight of the world's thirty highest peaks. K2 is the second highest mountain in the world, but is considered to be the most difficult to climb. It is known as 'the mountaineers' mountain', being on average 20 per cent steeper than Everest and, at 877km/545 miles further north, much colder. K2 has also been christened 'the savage mountain', partly due to its severe, fast-changing weather, but also for its high fatality rate: 27 per cent of the people who have climbed K2 have died on the descent, three times the rate on Mount Everest.

Climbers moving up to the most dangerous section on the mountain – the Bottleneck and Traverse – on the morning of 1 August 2008.

The Bottleneck, the start of the final approach to the summit, is not only extremely steep, it is also dangerously positioned beneath a serac about 90m/300ft high. A serac is a huge block of ice, often house-sized or bigger, formed by intersecting crevasses on a glacier. They are dangerous to mountaineers since they may topple or avalanche without warning, especially if they form an ice face on a hanging glacier, as is the case above the Bottleneck and Traverse on K2. Fixed ropes had been attached to metal screws in the ice earlier that morning to form a guideline for the climbers and allow them to clip in and reduce the risk of a fall as they ascended the near-vertical gully.

While Ger had been acclimatising to the altitude on K2, at home in Ireland his mother had been lighting candles for her son in a nearby church. Ger's sisters and his brother had been texting him with all the local news and goings on. Ger loved to hear about life in Kilcornan, County Limerick, while he was away on trips.

Not until the days before the summit attempt was there a mention in the Irish press about Ger's summit push. 'Limerick man close to summit history' read one paper. The McDonnell family ignored the hype, however, and silently prayed that Ger would achieve his dream and, most importantly, get home to tell them of his adventures. Ger never really liked briefing the press on his adventures; he would never refuse an interview but felt embarrassed to have his stories printed. He did what he did for the love of mountaineering. For Ger McDonnell this was the near completion of the dream of a lifetime. At thirty-seven years of age he was about to become the first Irishman to scale the summit of K2.

In 2008 there were ten international expeditions and various independent climbers on the mountain. Initially thirty-one people were pushing for the summit on 1 August, an unusually large number for K2, as the weather had not previously been suitable and the climbing season was about to end. It was now or never. An ad hoc meeting held at Base Camp when the weather window became apparent had agreed that a lead party, consisting of the strongest and most experienced climbers, sherpas (mountain guides from Nepal) and HAPs (high-altitude porters from Pakistan) would leave two hours before the main party to fix ropes on the Bottleneck and the next section of mountain, the dangerous Traverse, to speed up the ascent. Each person had been given a specific job to do, such as carry ropes, other climbing gear or bamboo sticks with flags to mark the route.

However, on summit day, the most experienced HAP, the only person who had previously placed ropes on the summit's approaches, became ill at Camp 2 and had to descend to Base Camp. Others dropped out of the advance party due to tiredness. The five remaining people in the advance group carried on, but started placing the fixed ropes too low down. When rope ran out, these lower ropes had to be removed and passed up the line to where they were needed, on the Traverse beyond the Bottleneck, causing delay and congestion in a situation where time was of the essence.

The Basque climber Alberto Zerain, who had come straight up from Camp 3 climbing independently, took charge of fixing the ropes along the Traverse section beyond the Bottleneck. Meanwhile, just before 8 a.m., at the start of the Bottleneck, which was ironically living up to its nickname, the climbers, most of whom had been climbing since 4.30 a.m., were caught in a queue, and running two to three hours late. At this point members of the American expedition, which included Eric Meyer, an anaesthetist with expertise in medical problems caused by high altitude, Chris Klinke and the Swede Fredrik

Pemba Gyalje at K2 Base Camp.

Strang, calculated that if they continued to the summit, they would have to climb down the Bottleneck in the dark, and reluctantly aborted their summit attempt for safety reasons, deciding to stay at Camp 4.

Wilco used the delay below the Bottleneck at 8,300m/27,231ft to rest and drink tea. He also sorted through his gear and took with him only his cameras and a litre of water, stuffed into his down suit. He hung his rucksack on the rocks, to retrieve on his return. This is done by many climbers to lighten their load as they push for the summit, because things are heavier in thin air, and every measure that preserves the climber's energy must be taken. The other members of the Dutch expedition pushing for the summit, besides Ger and Wilco, were Wilco's long-term climbing partner, Cas van de Gevel, and Pemba Gyalje. Pemba, who had been a member of the advance party, was up ahead at this point, and Cas and Ger were nearby, waiting to take their place on the rope and climb the Bottleneck.

The queue ground to a complete stop, and Wilco ran out of patience. He unclipped himself from the rope, and scrambled up a parallel snow gully, overtaking a number of climbers. Cecilie Skog, the leader of the Norwegian expedition, generously invited him by a gesture to clip on to the rope in front of her. When Wilco finally reached the top of the Bottleneck, he found his teammate Pemba, who explained that the delay was due to the slowness of the Korean expedition up ahead. The plans to avoid this situation by fixing the ropes early had failed. As Wilco fastened himself back on to the rope, he heard a loud scream and turned to see the Serbian climber Dren Mandić, only three metres away from him, fall backwards and down the mountain. Wilco lunged to try and catch him, but he was too late. Dren had temporarily unfastened himself from the rope to fix his oxygen supply, lost his balance and now lay about 400m/1,300ft below on a glacier.

The climbers were all in a state of shock at the sudden and probably fatal accident to one of their number, but despair was replaced by hope when the tiny figure below was seen to move. Jehan Baig, a Pakistani HAP, decided to descend immediately to offer aid, but did so in such a dangerous manner that Cas, who was nearby, was compelled to warn him that he was behaving recklessly. The Serbian climbers abandoned their summit attempt and started down to go to the aid of their compatriot. At the same time Klinke, Meyer and Strang from the American expedition heard the scream from Camp 4, saw the fallen body in the snow above them and made their way back up to offer help. But it was too late; when they and the Serbians reached Dren Mandić he was dead. The Serbians decided to bring the body down with the aid of the American expedition, but within moments the HAP Jehan Baig, whose careless behaviour on the descent suggested that the high-altitude lack of oxygen had impaired his judgement, lost his balance and, making no effort to halt his descent, fell to his death. He had almost taken the rest of the party with him, leaving them badly shaken, and so they reluctantly tied Dren Mandić's body to an ice axe and left his remains on the mountain.

The climbers on the Bottleneck and above it (still unaware of Jehan Baig's fatal fall) were all deeply dismayed at the sudden loss of Dren Mandić. Many were debating their next move, not only because of the Serbian's accident, but also because the window of time for reaching the summit and returning safely in daylight was rapidly narrowing. It was already 4 p.m., and it would take at least two to three hours more to reach the summit. It would be dark by around 8 p.m. Both Ger and Pemba, his highly experienced climbing companion, had doubts about continuing. Pemba later recalled feeling that the vibes were not good, a gut feeling also experienced by the American climber Chris Klinke, who had already abandoned his summit attempt. Ger, while naturally shocked by the loss of Dren Mandić, was very aware of the risks at that altitude. Speaking in a radio interview some years earlier he had said, 'Things go wrong, and when they do, these things are held under a microscope and people tend to criticise. They say ... they should or shouldn't have done this. There are a lot of people alive today that criticise and don't realise just how close they themselves have been to tragedy. It only takes the slightest thing to go wrong, or be delayed, and those people could have ended up in the same situation.

Marco Confortola on the Traverse.

Because you survive the mountain doesn't make you an expert. It doesn't give you a right to say someone made a mistake. When you weren't there you don't know – only the mountain knows the full story.'

The exceptionally fast Basque climber Alberto Zerain had already set off for the summit. As he waited above the Bottleneck for others he had been getting cold, so he decided to head for the summit alone. Many of the climbers at this point were anxious over just how late things were running and started to consider their options. Some felt it was already too late to go on, but the Italian climber Marco Confortola, a 37-year-old professional guide in the Alps, made an impassioned speech reminding his colleagues that the first men to conquer K2, an Italian expedition in 1954, had reached the summit at 6 p.m. 'If they could do it, so can we,' he later told *The Sunday Times*. Because there were fixed ropes on the most dangerous parts of the climb, there was less reason to fear descending in the dark.

At this stage Ger, Pemba, Wilco and Cas were all standing at the top of the Bottleneck on steep rocks. The next section of the mountain was possibly the most dangerous on K2. It is known as the Traverse and extends diagonally across a wall of sheer ice for approximately 250m/820ft, beneath overhanging seracs which Wilco described as being the size of multi-storey apartment blocks or cathedrals. In the Bottleneck climbers have a degree of protection from ice and rock falls, but on the Traverse they are completely exposed and would not survive an ice fall. Ger, who had suffered a fractured skull from a rock fall on his previous stint on K2, was still hesitating when the expedition leader Wilco clipped on to the rope and set off across the Traverse. To his right were vertical ice walls, so tall that he could not see their tops, while around 3m/10ft to his left was a vertical drop into an abyss some 3km/2 miles below. Ahead of Wilco was one of the slow Koreans. When he paused to look back he was glad to see that the other three members of the Dutch expedition heading for the summit that day were all following him: Cas, Ger and Pemba.

At the top of the Traverse Wilco sat and rested while the others caught up. He took a drink from his precious litre of water but while fumbling to close the bottle it slipped through his gloved hands. By now he was exhausted and the others overtook him. He was encouraged on his way by the Norwegian climbers, Cecilie and Lars, who were already on their way down from the summit. The third Norwegian climber, Rolf Bae, Cecilie's husband, was waiting for them at the top of the Traverse. Rolf had been having a bad day on the mountain and did not feel up to the final push to the top.

On 1 August 2008 at around 6.40 p.m., after seventeen hours of climbing and less than two hours after leaving the top of the Traverse, Gerard McDonnell made history by becoming the first Irishman to reach the summit of K2, fulfilling his dream. Pemba was by his side. They waited twenty minutes for Cas and then Wilco to join them. By that point Wilco was so exhausted that he was crawling on all fours, but once he reached his companions there were hugs and dancing, as well as tears. They were at the highest point of a surrounding range of mountains all at least 7,000m/23,000ft high. Wilco observed that the shadow of K2's summit could be seen stretching to the horizon; Camp 4, which they had left in the early morning, was so far down that it looked like a pinhead. Wilco found the magnificence of the vast snowy panorama so impressive that it left him light-headed.

Next to arrive was Hugues d'Aubarède, a 61-year-old Frenchman on his third and, he had declared, final K2 expedition, with his Pakistani climbing companion, Karim. Cas noticed that Hugues' oxygen bottle was empty due to the long delay on the Bottleneck.

Wilco called the expedition's webmaster Maarten van Eck at the base camp in the Netherlands to give him the news of the team's great achievement: 'Maarten! We are standing on K2!' Ger tried to call his mother from the summit but interference prevented this although he did get through to his girlfriend, Annie Starkey, in Anchorage, Alaska; both Ger and Annie were delighted, but knew the job was only half complete. Getting down to a safe camp is always the hardest part, but at that moment Ger was elated and feeling

Pemba Gyalje and Ger on the summit of K2. (Courtesy Wilco Van Rooijen)

Gerard McDonnell, the first Irishman to reach the summit, on top of K2 on 1 August 2008.

Team members congratulate each other on the summit of K2, 1 August 2008, (l–r) Hugues d'Aubarède, Karim Meherban, Wilco van Rooijen (in orange suit), Ger (in red and black suit) and Pemba Gyalje. (Courtesy Wilco van Rooijen)

Rolf Bae on the Antarctic Peninsula on 14 November 2006.

strong. At the end of the call, Annie asked him to be careful on the way down.

Ger insisted on waiting for Marco, the lone Italian climber, who was the last to reach the summit. Cas and Wilco recalled that they were on the summit for at least thirty minutes before Marco arrived, weak but elated. Prolonged hours at such a high altitude were taking their toll on them physically. Marco asked Cas to take some pictures of him, and called his sponsor to tell him the great news. It was now close to 8 p.m. local time and growing dark. The group had been on the summit for over an hour. But they had headlamps and there were fixed ropes; it was just a matter of staying awake and concentrating on the job in hand; they should be back in the safety of Camp 4 within three to four hours.

Back home in Ireland news had reached Ger's family that he had succeeded in getting to the summit of K2. While they knew a difficult descent was ahead of him, they were delighted to hear that he had achieved his dream. It was 2.30 p.m. Irish time. Celebrations were put on hold, however, until the family knew Ger had reached a safe camp.

On K2 all the climbers were descending slowly and some stopped to rest, after building a rudimentary 'seat' in the snow. It was now after 9 p.m. and dark, so Pemba decided to trail break with another sherpa, leaving two other sherpas to encourage the climbers. As Pemba reached the top of the Traverse, he looked up and down but couldn't find the fixed rope. As he looked up again, he suddenly realised that the serac they had passed beneath earlier in the day had sheared from the ice wall and taken the fixed lines with it. This was a major disaster. Without the fixed lines in place, the returning climbers were in serious trouble. Pemba tried to contact Wilco and the rest of the team on the radio, but did not get a response.

Only later did Pemba find out that not only had the fixed lines been lost, but a climber had been carried away with them. At approximately 7.45 p.m. Cecilie, the 34-year-old leader of the Norwegian team, on her way down from the summit with Lars, met up with her husband Rolf, who had not attempted the summit. He was delighted at the achievement of his wife and teammate and there were hugs all round. Then they started across the Traverse in the dark with only their head torches for guidance. Rolf was first on the fixed line. As Cecilie was due to go on the line she suddenly heard a familiar noise, the scratching of ice. When climbers describe avalanches or serac falls, they often compare the sound that heralds the fall to a scratching noise. The avalanche from the serac swept past her and carried Rolf away. Cecilie called out in desperation and tried to find her husband with her headlamp, but she already knew in her heart that he was gone forever. The unthinkable had happened, and she felt the first terrible pangs of grief. But she also knew she had to stay focused on survival, get down the mountain and tell the world what had happened to her beloved Rolf.

The fixed line had been cut some 50–80m/165–260ft above the start of the Traverse, with its sickening drop into the abyss on one side. But the well-prepared Norwegians were carrying spare lightweight rope, even though they knew there would be fixed lines, and they used their spare rope, crampons and ice axes to climb down. As they descended they called frantically for Rolf, but there was no reply. They arrived in Camp 4 between 10 and 11 p.m, Cecilie distraught at her loss.

Pemba and Chhiring Dorje, realising that the ropes were gone, decided to continue down using crampons and ice axes. They were exhausted after a long day and had been at high altitude for too long. It was too dark to search for the other climbers. The most sensible thing to do was return to a lower altitude to rest and recover before beginning to search the next day. Their descent in the dark without fixed ropes was not only highly skilful, in one case it was also heroic. Sherpa Pasang Lama had used his ice axe to set up a belay earlier in the day, and no one had a spare. Chhiring Dorje, a sherpa who owned a Kathmandu-based guide service and had stood on the summit of Everest ten times, was probably the most experienced high-altitude climber on K2 on that fateful day. When he realised his colleague's predicament, he tied Sherpa Pasang Lama to his harness with a sling, and then, facing in, calmly climbed down using only crampons and ice axe, with his colleague attached. One slip and they would both have fallen into the abyss. This was at 8,230m/27,000 ft, in the middle of the night, after Chhiring Dorje had reached the summit of K2 without oxygen.

Wilco, who had stopped for a power nap in a snow seat he dug for himself, became separated from his fellow expedition members. Pemba had successfully descended, and Cas also managed to climb down the Traverse and the Bottleneck in the dark. On his way he met the Frenchman Hugues who had run out of oxygen and become separated from his climbing companion Karim, who had been complaining of fatigue on the summit. Hugues, who was looking tired, waved the faster climber Cas past. Shortly afterwards, when Cas had reached the bottom of the Bottleneck, he heard a scratching noise. When he turned around, he saw Hugues falling past him to his death in an avalanche. Shocked and exhausted, Cas stumbled into Camp 4 where he met Pemba. The Korean expedition leader Kim Jae-soo managed to get down the Bottleneck in the dark and sent rescuers to help his female teammate Go Mi-sun who was unsure of which route to follow. At dawn the next morning there were still eight climbers on the mountain above Camp 4 unaccounted for: three Koreans, their sherpas, Jumik Bhote, Karim Meherban (Hugues' climbing partner), Marco the Italian, Wilco and Ger.

That evening, Ger's family kept a vigil by both phone and Internet, for what felt like an eternity, waiting for news of Ger's progress. News broke that an accident had occurred on K2 and two climbers were dead. Information was very sketchy and the details of what had happened to Dren Mandić and Jehan Baig were not yet known but the first seeds of serious worry were planted. Hopes were still high among the McDonnell family that Ger would be accounted for shortly – they knew nothing of the plight of the climbers who were now trapped above the Bottleneck, without a fixed line or spare ropes, in the dark. For the next eighteen hours Denise (Ger's sister and my wife) and the rest of the family sought news on the Norit website and spoke to Annie by phone. They also tried to contact Maarten, the Norit webmaster, for answers. All night the website remained unchanged: Ger's status was given as 'unknown'. By Saturday afternoon a group of friends and family had gathered at Ger's sister Martha's home to support the family and wait for news. Neighbours and friends took turns making tea and sandwiches, while Ger's brother J. J., who had been on a week's holiday in the sun to celebrate his birthday with his girlfriend Céren, got the earliest flight home.

2. ARRIVAL IN PAKISTAN (AND BUILD-UP FOR DENALI CLIMB)

The Norit K2 Dutch International Expedition (as it was officially called) arrived in Islamabad in May 2008, two months before the summit bid, in order to acclimatise. Wilco, along with Cas van de Gevel, his long-term climbing partner, Roeland van Oss, Court Haegens and Jelle Staleman, made up the Dutch members of the team. Wilco and Cas knew Ger from his 2006 attempt on K2, when he had retired due to a serious head injury. It was through Ger that Pemba was part of the Norit K2 climb. 'Early in 2007 he sent me an exciting email,' Pemba recalls. 'He told me "I want to climb K2 again in 2008 from a different route, I love that mountain."' In 2006 Ger had failed to persaude Pemba to join him on K2, as his family obected to the idea of Pemba tackling a mountain with such a dangerous reputation. He made it clear that Pemba was being invited on the 2008 expedition as a fully sponsored expedition member, not 'as an altitude worker or climbing sherpa'. This time the family relented and Pemba gave up his Everest expedition that season and prepared to go to Pakistan. Ger organised everything for his trip through the Norit team. Sometimes the western media and climbers have been accused of not giving the same respect and coverage to sherpa climbers, and this was something that Ger often discussed with Pemba.

The sherpas are an ethnic group from the highest region of the Himalayas in Nepal and are famous as mountain guides. Their contribution has been recognised ever since New Zealander Sir Edmund Hillary first stood on the summit of Everest with the most famous sherpa of all, Tenzing Norgay.

Climbing friends (l–r): Mark Sheen, Jelle Staleman, Marco Confortola, Ger and Cas van de Gevel.
(Courtesy Wilco van Rooijen)

Because the sherpas are born at high altitude they have adapted genetically to the thin air, and have more strength, speed and stamina than European and American climbers. Ger first encountered sherpas during his 2003 expedition to Everest. 'After that he become a fan of sherpas because he respected the sherpa contribution on high-altitude mountains,' says Pemba. 'Gerard was always telling me, he was not satisfied with the western mountaineering community because they still don't properly evaluate the sherpa contribution on the mountains.'

Ger was delighted to have Pemba back climbing with him and there is no doubt the respect was mutual. To Pemba, Ger was 'True Mountain' and someone who loved adventure, but who was also a pure and unselfish climber. They discussed making a film together about the sherpas' mountaineering skills as they felt there was no proper documentary film on the subject, but for now they were just glad to be back climbing together. Australian Mark Sheen was also well known to Ger from the previous K2 expedition in 2006, when Mark was climbing Broad Peak, the mountain Ger and his team were using to acclimatise for K2. It was largely because of Ger that Mark had decided to join the K2 expedition, having kept in touch since 2006. They were reunited when Mark answered a knock on the door to his hotel room in Islamabad to find a smiling Ger standing there: 'G'day Sheeny.'

Mark Sheen's first recollections of Ger in 2006 were very different.

At the time I was inexperienced with those kind of altitudes and also this was my first time on an 8,000m/26,000ft peak. Not only that, I had not done any mountaineering for several years and most of my expedition and climbing gear was old and heavy. On this expedition there were several climbers who were very experienced, amazingly fit and determined. Ger was one of those climbers. I felt in awe but also out of place beside them in the climbing sense. Should I be here, I thought, but then how am I to learn? In the course of the expedition Ger stood out as the person who offered his experience and didn't mind sharing his knowledge.

Peaks of over 8,000m/26,000ft are the ultimate challenge to serious mountain climbers. There are only fourteen mountain peaks over this range, all of them in the Himalaya and Karakoram ranges. The great Italian mountaineer Reinhold Messner was the first to climb all fourteen peaks. It took him sixteen years and he completed the climbs in 1986 aged forty-two. American Ed Viesturs became the first American to climb all fourteen in May 2005. Both agreed that K2, second only to Everest in height at 8,611m/28,251ft, was both the most beautiful and the most challenging of all the tall peaks. All climbers on K2, whether on an official expedition or climbing independently, need to submit details of their climbing experience to the authorities in Pakistan before receiving a permit to climb on the mountain. K2 has not experienced the surge in commercial expeditions which has turned the Everest experience into one which can be 'bought'. As Ed Viesturs says in the first chapter of his book, *K2: Life and Death on the World's Most Dangerous Mountain*, the reason for this lack of commercialisation is quite simply because K2 is so difficult to climb.

Wilco survived his ordeal on K2 and wrote a book about it, *Surviving K2*, which he dedicated to Gerard McDonnell. In this he highlights the dangers of high-altitude climbing by pointing out that if a human being is taken from sea level to 8,000m/26,000ft directly, that person will die in minutes. Climbers increasingly refer to heights over 8,000m as 'the death zone', where the height is so extreme that no human body can acclimatise. The time a climber can spend at this height is strictly limited, as there is not enough oxygen in the air to sustain human life. The bodily functions start to deteriorate, leading to loss of consciousness and death. As each individual's tolerance of high altitude varies, there is no hard and fast rule as to how long you can expect to survive at extreme high altitude, but it would normally be measured in hours rather than days. Careful, slow acclimitisation to altitude helps to increase one's tolerance. Death can occur through loss of vital functions or indirectly through bad decisions made due to mental confusion caused by lack of oxygen to the brain (hypoxia) and general weakness. Climbers at high altitude are prone to becoming hypoxic, that is to say, mentally confused and physically clumsy, and constantly monitor each other for these signs, which can be alleviated by heading for a lower altitude.

Medical experts recognise three regions of altitude: high altitude at 1,500–3,500m/4,900–11,500ft; very high altitude at 3,500m–5,500m/11,500ft–18,000ft; and extreme altitude which is above 5,500m/18,000ft. Each region can lead to medical problems varying from altitude sickness (headache, dehydration, dizziness, fatigue, nausea and/or vomiting) to the potentially fatal conditions of pulmonary oedema (fluid in the lungs) and cerebral oedema (swelling of the brain).

One of the most unpleasant aspects of high-altitude acclimatisation are the digestive problems encountered. The body prioritises more important functions, primarily the working of the heart and lungs, and the digestive capability is severely diminshed, which can lead to diarrhoea and frequent bouts of vomiting – Ger referred to the latter cheerfully as 'decorating the snow'.

Ger's Training for High-Altitude Ascents

Ger had vivid memories of his early training and acclimatisation climbs for his first big peak. Living in Alaska nine years earlier, in 1999, he was hoping to attempt the highest peak in America, Mount McKinley, or Denali as it is known to the locals. To that end he had undertaken mountaineering and winter survival courses to add to his general climbing experience but he also needed to get in some training climbs. With a group of friends Ger decided to attempt a mountain called Marcus Baker in the Chugach mountain range. Their intention was to climb it over a long weekend. By Alaskan standards it was not a very high mountain, just over 4,000m/13,000ft. Due to its geographical location, there is a lot of rain in winter and a lot of snow in summer. As luck would have it, Ger's climb coincided with the three worst recorded storms in the area's history, as he recounts in his log for March 1999.

There we were on the mountain being hit with storm after storm and our intention was to climb it over a long weekend and two weeks later we're still there! Interesting times. We had extra supplies of food, which we buried in the snow for storage, but it snowed so much we couldn't get to the food, it was completely buried ...

Things were bad now; we had our provisions buried, we lost one tent, a few guys were frostbitten and one guy Jeff [Jessen] was hypothermic, and mobile reception was poor and weak on the mountain. Luckily one guy who worked as a park ranger had a lot of contacts and when we eventually got coverage he called the rescue rangers where he worked and called in a rescue. After this call was made there was a division in the camp – one guy said he did not want a rescue and he didn't want his name in the paper!

My own opinion is that if a guy needs rescue he needs rescue; who am I to say 'hey look, you're fine'. It was everyone for themselves as we didn't have a leader as such, as it normally isn't required for the smaller peaks. At the end of the day the plane arrived to rescue three guys, two who were frostbitten and Jeff who was hypothermic. We watched as the plane took off and as it did we noticed it coming down again in a cloud of snow! We thought they had crashed. Now there were only two of us left on the mountain but when the plane took off again and circled we noticed that it was only the pilot. The plane couldn't take off with the three lads, so a decision had to be made as to who was going. It could take two but not three. They ended up playing rock-paper-scissors to decide their fate. Jeff, the guy who was hypothermic, lost and he was disgusted with himself. 'I chose paper after scissors; you never do that!'

Americans claim that there's a skill involved in rock-paper-scissors. The other two lads then headed off in the plane. That night we got in contact with the rescue ranger; we told him our situation and he said, 'Well it's like this, whatever storms you've experienced it's nothing compared to what you're about to experience!' That revelation shook us and we started to dig much deeper and faster; we dug out a snow cave to protect us from the 100 mph wind and the -40 degrees chill factor. It was turning so cold that you could get a cup of boiling water and throw it up in the air and it would vaporise before it hit the ground.

Jeff grabs the phone and says, 'Right that's it, I'm calling in rescue.' He goes outside and he says, 'Hi lads, it's Jeff, one of the guys on Marcus Baker – I'm calling rescue, we need you guys to help us.'

We were still in tents at this point and planned to stay there as long as we could, as it is a lot warmer in the tents. Outside we heard Jeff talking. 'Oh right so – okay. We're just tired! Yeah, okay, bye!' he hangs up and this is followed by a lot of swearing.

The reason they couldn't pick us up was that 100 miles over in Cordova a bunch of guys on snow mobiles were after being killed in an avalanche but Jeff was so mad he said that if they're hit by an avalanche they'll most likely be all dead, do we need to be dead before they rescue us?

Ger and his fellow climbers made it off Marcus Baker but perhaps it was experiences like this that led to him being more open with his knowledge to climbers like Mark Sheen over the years. Even in these early climbs the adventurer in him and his great sense of fun and humour were evident, as his close friend Jeff Jessen recalls.

I first met Ger in an outdoor gear store in Anchorage, Alaska, called REI which means Recreational Equipment Incorporated. Ger probably talked a lot about this place as he spent a lot of time and money here getting gear for his adventures and future expeditions. Ger was such a friendly guy that when he would come into the store quite often I'd start chatting to him and try to find out his stories.

I remember one day in particular I started chatting just about hiking in Alaska to Gerard and taking trips into the wilderness … and I said, 'Hey maybe we could do some hikes together?' So from there we decided that we'd head off on a couple of local hikes together to see just how we would get along, and of course to see how were our own abilities to explore.

Ger, I and Mike Thompson, another friend of ours who was a ranger, the three of us started doing some local climbs together and as we talked further during those hikes we all expressed an interest in doing a bit of mountaineering; neither Ger nor I really had much climbing done at this point. Gerard and I both said, 'Yeah, it would be really cool to go up Denali some time.' We all agreed it was something we should aim at and that we would start planning for the spring of 1999.

We spent the whole fall of '98 right up to the spring of our departure in May 1999 doing preliminary trips and training in everything from winter camping to building snow caves, glacier training and rescue classes. We did it all! I think that we took it pretty seriously. The really neat thing about Gerard was that when he got his mind into something he would go out and source the right gear and get all the proper stuff. I suppose it was one of the many things I admired about Ger that there were no half measures with him.

So we ended up doing a variety of trips to the build-up; the preliminary trips we did were Bold Peak [a 2,292m/7,520ft mountain in Anchorage County in Alaska] and Mount Marcus Baker [a mountain in Matanuska-Susitna borough in Alaska standing 3,976m/13,045ft tall]. Marcus Baker was a huge mountain for us because we ended up getting stormed in for close to ten days. We did a bunch of several smaller trips which weren't all that serious but added to our experiences. I think these trips really bonded us together …

One of the best experiences I remember that really cemented our friendship was that Ger could make jokes and make fun out of a terrible situation. On one particular climb we were in a lot of heavy snow – basically up to our waist in snow, it was really deep – and Ger was the leader who would snow plough the way forward, or as we would say, break trail [in winter, to hike in the lead position, forcing your way through untrammeled snow. It is far easier to walk in the tracks of someone else who has already 'broken' the trail]. Ger had an incredible amount of strength and energy so it seemed easier for him to break trail and we would climb down after him. I remember Ger would always make light of the hard situation and say, 'Hey, this is just incredible!' He did everything in his power to make us laugh and I guess one characteristic about Ger that I'll never forget is his laugh; he had such a great, infectious laugh.

I remember on another trip, when we were near the summit we took off our backpacks (with these rucksacks you could unclip the top part and strap it around your waist like a bum bag and then head to the summit with a much lighter load). We would only have our cameras, water and energy bars to the summit. Just as we were about to shove off, [fellow climber] Mike Mays had his camera to place into the top part of his bag and had momentarily laid it down on the slope to adjust his crampon. He ended up knocking his bag down the slope and it kept rolling and rolling with Mike running after it and every time Mike thought it would stop it just kept rolling. At this stage both Ger and I got into an uncontrollable fit of laughter. It must have rolled down at least 1,000m.

Mike was more than a little upset with our reaction, but when we were finally able to contain ourselves Ger just said, 'Hey look, we'll just go down with you and get your gear and then give the summit another go.' That was just the kind of person Ger was, he didn't have an ego nor did it matter to him whether or not he got to the summit right there and then. He would always help out his teammates, so we travelled down with Mike and got his gear and turned around and just came right back up again. It made the day a heck of a lot longer but we all enjoyed it and it was really a great climb. Coming down we had already decided that we would do some camping overnight in a snow cave for training for Denali. We ended up building a snow cave up on the face of a hill on our descent. We spent the night or most of it in the cave.

For some reason it was extremely cold that night and as I only had a light sleeping bag I just couldn't sleep any more and decided I would head back off this mountain. To keep moving when you're cold like this is very important. Mike wanted to stay a bit longer in the cave so Ger said he would accompany me out. Ger and I hiked out till we got to the trail leading back to the car park. It was around November time and as we travelled out we saw this incredible display of northern lights.

Blues, reds, whites and greens – it was so amazing that we just lay in the middle of the trail and stared up at them for about half an hour. That was the beautiful thing about our relationship, that we would always take time to seek out the natural wonders that the world had to offer.

The world and its beauty was something Ger always spoke about; he often talked about Ireland to me and about how green it was. He would bring back stories from around the world about different environments, which was always important to him.

We both trekked out to the car park after the cold night in the cave. I was driving back to the highway and Ger was napping in the passenger seat beside me. He woke for a few minutes and said, 'Hey Jeff, maybe we should pull over for a nap for a while.' I remember saying, 'Yeah that's a great idea cause I'm really tired.' Ger looked up again and after about sixty seconds he sees that I'm sound asleep behind the wheel! He jumps over, grabs the wheel and screams, 'Jeff, wake up – you're asleep!' We ended up pulling over at the next opportunity and we both slept for about an hour. We always laughed about that night …'

Charles B. Roberts was on another training climb for Denali:

> Ger was in the process of training for his climb on Mount McKinley, or Denali as some people call it. Ger had asked me if I wanted to join him, Mike and Jeff for a hike up a particular ridge, the name escapes me at this time. The training occurred during February or March, so you can imagine it was cold, probably around -10 °F (-23 °C) and that didn't include the wind-chill. I do remember it being so cold that when I was putting my boots on, for that brief moment, prior to beginning to hike, my fingers had turned to ice cubes. I could not feel them. So we go up, making our way, he, Mike and Jeff practising certain self-arresting techniques, certain situations they may run into, roping themselves up, helping each other around obstacles, even some avalanche training. Well, we get to the summit, have our photo op and we are ready to descend down to the cars. Ger, Mike, and Jeff had snow shovels they were carrying and Jeff and Ger decide, hey, why don't we ride these down instead of hiking all that way. I thought they were nuts. I could only imagine how fast they would get going on that somewhat hard-packed snow. Well, sure enough, I believe Jeff went first. He slowly straddled the handle and placed his butt right on the business end of the shovel. I even think that a couple of us had to hold on to him until the count of three. We got to two and he took off like a rocket! Screaming down the hillside. Well, Ger had to try also. Of course, Ger did it with style. He mounted the same as Jeff and let it fly. He lasted a whole three seconds before pulling the shovel from underneath him and digging his mountain axe into the snow as his rudder. What a sight! I thought there could have been an Olympic sport of this. Ger, of course, would have gotten the gold.

In May 1999, the three team members set off for their adventure on Denali, none of them knowing what to expect. Ger, who funded his own climb, also used the opportunity to raise awareness (and funds) to support a local hospice at home in Ireland. With the help of his family, he had organised a campaign to raise money for Milford Hospice, a cancer-care unit in Limerick that supports the terminally ill and their families. The hospice is partially funded by the state, but has to balance its books through donations and fund-raising. With the generous help of the local community, Ger's family organised a dance in the local hall and family and close friends collected sponsorship door to door in Kilcornan and the surrounding parishes. Together they raised the impressive sum of £15,000 for the hospice.

3. THE TREK TO K2 BASE CAMP (AND GER'S EARLY YEARS)

K2, May 2008

To reach Askole, the starting point for the trek to Base Camp at K2, climbers must take a two-day bus journey, 793km/493 miles from Islamabad to Skardu. The tedium of the journey is alleviated by spectacular mountain views including the peaks of Nanga Parbat at 8,125m/26,656ft and Rakaposhi at 7,790m/25,558ft. From Skardu the expedition continues in FJ40 Land Cruisers for a dangerous, off-road drive of 110km/68 miles to Askole where porters are hired and the trek itself begins.

From this point on, all communication equipment is powered by solar energy, and there are no more villages or settlements at which to buy food and drink. From Askole the expedition was accompanied by its porters, who had spent an entertaining and efficient couple of hours inspecting the gear once it had been unloaded from the Land Cruisers. One by one they had come forward to choose the 25kg load of their liking. When organising the expedition, Wilco and the sponsors, Norit, had contracted a local company to supply porters and tents, and cooking and other staff to man the base camp for the duration of their stay. The expedition also travelled with an impressive array of communications equipment including satellite phone to keep in touch with Maarten van Eck, the webmaster at their base back in the Netherlands. Maarten would not only ensure that news of the expedition's progress reached the outside world by updating the website and keeping its press officers briefed, he was also in charge of supplying the expedition with specialised meteorological reports that would help the climbers to plan their summit attempt. The medical hotline to the expedition's doctor also went via Maarten.

The Norit team in Skardu *(l–r):* Cas van de Gevel, Roeland van Oss, Norit walking member, Ger, Jelle Staleman, Wilco van Rooijen, Norit walking member, Mark Sheen, Pemba Gyalje, Norit walking member. (Courtesy Wilco van Rooijen).

Ger and his companions were delighted to stretch their legs after the long bus and off-road journey, and begin the seven-day trek to base camp, and the long process of acclimatisation to altitude. Askole is at 2,500m/8,200ft but the trekkers would quickly climb to 5,000m/16,400ft. Unfortunately the first six-hour hike to Camp Jhula ended in a mild dust storm. Because of his asthma, Ger was glad to have a dust mask, but he was on the receiving end of some ribbing from his fellow team members for wearing it. Ger was always careful to look after himself health-wise; heat and dust caused problems with his asthma. Wearing the dust mask enabled him to carry on walking through the storm. And now there was the novelty of setting up camp in a dust storm. Over the next seven days of six- to eight-hour hikes (with one day of rest) they would advance towards the base camp from which to launch their assault on K2.

Setting out from Camp Jhula the expedition resumed its trek along the Braldu River to a green oasis under the shadows of Paiju peak, which stands at 6,611m/21,690ft. Paiju is a Balti word meaning 'salt', derived from the fact there are rock salt deposits at the base of this peak. Some of the locals believe that the snow on the summit of Paiju Peak is not snow but a huge deposit of salt, which drips down to the base.

Ger (in yellow T-shirt) at the junction point of the Hindu Kush, the Karakoram and the Himalaya.
(Courtesy Wilco van Rooijen)

The first view of the magnificent K2 is usually (depending on the weather) from the Baltoro Glacier. Climber after climber has reported their initial view of K2 as a combination of awe at its size and wonder at the sheer beauty of the huge mountain, its iconic peak soaring 8km/5 miles above sea level, often wreathed in wisps of cloud. The huge flanks of its lower slopes consist of a formidable combination of rock and ice, while its higher slopes are coated in pristine snow.

The next day the expedition crossed the junction of the magnificent Paiju and Baltoro Glaciers through crevasses, taking lunch in a camp under the muddy cliffs of Liligo with views of rock spires. They then crossed the Khuburse torrent and rambled over two glacier moraines to reach the grassy slopes of Urdukas offering splendid views of the Trango and Uli Biaho mountains where they camped for the night, now at 4,130m/13,550ft. The next day a long walk on the Baltoro Glacier lay in front of them. From there they had to cross over another glacier, which flows down from the Masherbrum and joins the Baltoro. The reward for this tough six to seven hours of hiking

At the town of Askole, porters wait to take their choice of load from the equipment. (Courtesy Wilco van Rooijen).

Sorting gear at Base Camp on K2 (*l–r*): Ger, Cas van de Gevel, Pemba Gyalje, Roeland van Oss and Mark Sheen. (Courtesy Wilco van Rooijen)

was magnificent views of the Muztagh, Mitre and Gasherbrum mountains. Here at 4,500m/14,800ft, twice as high as Askole, and just under half the height of K2's 8,611m/28,251ft summit, the group spent another night in tents. Next morning they resumed the long hike up the Baltoro Glacier to a point called Concordia – the junction of the Baltoro, Abruzzi and Godwin Austin Glaciers. Within a short radius of 15km/9 miles stand forty-one peaks over 6,500m/21,300ft, including four peaks above 8,000m/26,000ft, offering a breathtaking, snowy panorama not to be found anywhere else on earth. In the midst of this spectacular view Ger and his fellow climbers camped at 4,720m/15,500ft, then took a day's rest to aid acclimatisation. The next day, 29 May 2008, they made the short four-hour hike to the K2 Base Camp at 4,650m/15,250ft. To their great satisfaction, the Norit K2 Dutch International Expedition were the first to arrive at base camp for the 2008 season, and had the pick of the best locations for their mess tent, latrines and overnight tents.

Ger's Early Years

Gerard McDonnell was born to Gertie and Denis, dairy farmers, on 20 January 1971 in Kilcornan, a parish of about 1,125 people 20km/12 miles west of Limerick on the N69, south of the Shannon estuary. The most famous landmark near the parish is Curraghchase Forest Park, part of which is a public amenity that includes tourist trails, camping and caravan park facilities.

Ger enjoying the outdoors at a very young age.

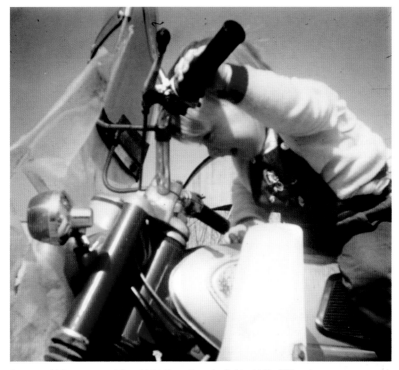

Two-year-old Ger on a motorbike, which belonged to a family friend Mike O'Shaughnessy.

Ger (back row, third from left) proudly lines out with the Kilcornan football team – they were West Limerick Champions 1985–86.

The parish of Kilcornan is physically not unlike many another small parish in rural Ireland, consisting of a church, a primary school, a community hall, a pub and a shop. GAA and soccer had always been a lynchpin of the community but due to the downturn in the economy, nowadays there isn't the same amount of young people to support the two organisations. The GAA is struggling, while the soccer is holding its own. Kilcornan is a special place in that the community is very close and neighbours are always on hand to help with whatever occasion presents itself, whether a happy or sad one.

The main business in Kilcornan is farming, while in nearby Askeaton (8km/5 miles west), where Ger attended secondary school, the two major employers are Aughinish Alumina and Pfizer (formerly Wyeth). Many locals commute to Limerick city to work.

The night of Ger's birth saw one of the fiercest storms in living memory, remembered by locals as the night a farmer from the outskirts of a nearby village was killed by a tree felled by lightning. It was on his parents' farm that Ger developed his early sense of adventure, roaming the farmland with his trusted dog Princess. His mother, Gertie, remembers that he was 'forever disappearing, and never in the same room as you. But all you had to do was call the dog and whatever direction he came from you could bank on Ger being in that general area.' Ger always believed that everyone was born with a love of climbing but that it was 'belted out of them as children' to get out of trees or down from the stairs. He soon found other pursuits to keep him occupied, but later in life he rediscovered that love for climbing and adventure.

During his years in the local primary school in Kilcornan, Ger was an active participant in sports and activities, representing the school in football and draughts in the 1981 Community Games. So it came as a bit of surprise when, during the summer of 1983, his mother noticed that Ger seemed to be caught for breath, not like someone who had just run a marathon, a different sort of shortness of breath. She kept an eye on him over the next few days but the condition did not seem to improve, so a trip to the local GP was followed by a trip to the hospital. Ger was diagnosed with asthma and was prescribed an inhaler. He was also told to stop using dairy products and start using soya milk. Right from the start, Ger seemed to be in full control of his new condition. He never let his asthma get the better of him, always involving himself in various sports and activities.

Ger played both Gaelic football and hurling throughout his school years for Kilcornan and was on winning under-16 championship teams in both codes. While climbing would take over later in life, Ger made no secret of the fact that he was passionate about hurling while growing up. In an interview

L–r: Tom Hanley, Ger McDonnell, Tom Downes, John Mulcair and J. J. McDonnell at St Brigid's Well in Kilcornan in 2005.

J. J., Ger and Stephanie enjoying the summer sun on the farm.

A McDonnell family portrait. Back row (l–r): Ger and J. J. Front row (l–r) Denis, Stephanie holding baby Denise, Martha and Gertie.

for West Limerick 102 local radio he joked that he had 'to give it up because it was too dangerous, I felt I had more control of the situation on the mountains than I did on a hurling field'.

School friends remember Ger developing something of a wild streak in secondary school in Askeaton, but while he mitched off on occasion, he took his studies seriously and wanted to do well in his exams. They remember his very active sense of humour but that he also had a serious and caring side to him. One friend, John Mulcair, recounts, 'I had a pretty bad stammer at school and it never really bothered Ger. In fact, he was very protective of me and when a certain guy was bullying me for a while I told Ger about it. Ger didn't mess about. He was incredibly fit and strong even then. He was very protective of people he cared for and he took things like that personally.'

It was obvious to his friend John that family was very important to Ger. 'He always talked about J. J. back then and really looked up to him; he was always very proud of J. J. and never once said a bad word about him. Even at school he made it clear that his family was very important to him. They came first.' J. J. was his brother and the eldest of the family, followed by Martha, born eighteen months later, then Stephanie eleven months after that. Ger was born four years after Stephanie and was followed by Denise eight years later, the baby of the clan. The McDonnells were a very close family with everyone pitching in to help around the house and farm. As the eldest, J. J. took on the responsibilities of helping on the farm. In 1987 when J. J. went to Australia for the year, Ger took his place, helping around the farm for the summer.

His final year at secondary school was looming and friends remember that 'he wanted to get good results in his exams'. All the hard work paid off and he achieved the results needed to study electronic engineering in Dublin City University (DCU). However, before going to college Ger and his two best friends, John Mulcair and Tommy Hanley, decided to spread their wings and head to England to work for the summer.

At seventeen, it was Ger's first big adventure away from home. After several attempts Ger and John Mulcair got jobs together on a building site; Ger was determined they would work together even though they could have secured jobs earlier had they been willing to split up. They enjoyed their summer in London, taking in the delights of the city and trying to chat up girls in Irish. The Kilcornan boys used to love speaking Irish on the underground or in pubs, knowing the locals couldn't understand. 'We used to tell the girls they were very sexy and we wanted to go off with them,' recalls John. 'They wouldn't understand a word but myself and Ger would be in fits of giggles.' Ger always kept in touch with home. One time he stayed up till 4 a.m. writing letters home, even though he was only away for six or seven weeks in total.

The following year Ger added to his travels by working in Greece for the summer. Failing to find regular work, he took to selling ice cream on the beaches. Even though Ger was not licensed to do so, he carried a large cooler box packed with various ice creams and when a figure of authority was spotted on the beach Ger would calmly sit on his box and suck on his ice cream and give them a cheerful salute. He returned to Ireland with a dinghy and spear gun he had picked up there.

To his family, Ger's sense of adventure was no surprise, having seen the seeds sown in his early years. Home from college one weekend, Ger borrowed his older brother's bike on the pretence of cycling the 8km/5 miles to Askeaton to post a letter. However, enjoying the cycle, he kept going until he ended up in west Clare, a mere 112km/70 miles away. When he stopped in a pub in

Doolin for a pint and a sandwich, he got talking to three local men at the bar. Naturally they asked where he was from and, on being told, they further enquired if he was down for the weekend. 'No,' said Ger, 'just cycled down for a pint and a sandwich.'

Ger's Early Climbing Days

In between his trips to England and Greece Ger had rediscovered his love of climbing when he joined the DCU rock-climbing club. 'I remember vividly my first rock climb ever, it was just really exciting ... there is a climber who says the art of rock climbing is relearning what you knew intuitively as a child. So I became addicted to it, I really enjoyed DCU rock climbing and ended up competing in various competitions.' College friends like Derry O'Donovan remember well Ger's love of climbing.

> Being short of money we had invented games to occupy our time, one of these was the stair Olympics. Basically this involved various physical feats around the stairs – climbing it without touching any steps, seeing how many steps you could jump down, etc. Ger, of course, took this a step further than anyone and ended up at a house party climbing out an upstairs window on one side of the house and climbing back in on the other.

Ger was also known as a practical joker in college. One of his housemates was an avid fan of *Twin Peaks*, and he always arrived home five minutes before an episode was due to begin to watch it on the TV in their upstairs apartment. One night Ger and the other students in the apartment took every piece of furniture and placed it at the bottom of the stairs. They then took the TV and put it up in the attic and climbed up there with it. When the housemate got back at 8.55 p.m. for the 9 p.m. episode, he was met with a wall of furniture. He managed to get through this, only to find that the TV was gone. On another occasion, in a house Ger lived in with a few others, one particular tenant refused to pay his share of the heating bill, claiming he had the radiator turned off in his room. One day Ger had to go up to this room and when the door was opened he was greeted by a blast of heat. Ger being Ger, he said nothing to the individual but swore to the others that he would play a trick on him some time soon. A few weeks later this individual was waiting for a job offer from a Japanese company and had asked Ger to pass on any phone messages he might have missed when he was out. Ger left a note telling him that a Japanese person called Mr Pin Okio had called and he had left a number. The number Ger gave him was the local Chinese takeaway and the guy ended up in a heated argument with the receptionist at the takeaway, who could not understand why this Irish guy wanted to speak with a fictional wooden character.

Family Tragedy and an Unexpected Opportunity

In 1991, halfway through the final year of Ger's degree course, tragedy struck when his father Denis died from a heart attack caused by a rare blood disorder. Devastated, Ger decided to take the rest of the year out from his studies. Returning to college the following year he successfully resat his exams and graduated from DCU as an electronic engineer. By chance his time in DCU was also to have a major impact on where he would go next in his life.

> I came into the canteen one day and there was a bunch of friends of mine madly filling out sheets of paper. Of course I asked them what they were doing and they replied that the deadline for the Morrison visa was tomorrow. I asked what it was and they explained it was the lottery visa system for the States. I never had any intention of going to the States but someone tore out a sheet of paper and pushed it in my direction, ordered me to fill it out and put down my name, address and a few bits of other information. A few months later I got something in the mail that said 'Congratulations, you have won a visa to the States' so that's how easy it was for me to get a green card, much to the chagrin of the other lads who had been trying for years to get it. I still wasn't too keen on moving to the States but the World Cup happened to be over there at the time and it coincided with having to go there to validate the visa, so I went over. I had my degree and decided to stay for a little while. Initially I went to Virginia – I stayed with my cousin and friend Ronan who is an airline pilot and also owned a carpet-cleaning business – later moving to Winchester, Virginia Beach, and I ended up in a software engineering job in Maryland.

Ger worked with Nucletron as a research and development software engineer until early 1997. At that point he was doing some hiking and 'a little bit of climbing every now and then'. But he started to get itchy feet again and was unsure of where to go next when:

> the boss at the time said a position had come up in Norway and asked me to come with him and offered me a job. I was delighted

Ger with his trusty bike, travelling across America.

because I was tired of the east coast and I was ready to leave. Saying yes to the job, I also requested a few months off to tour around North America. I had a motorcycle at the time and the plan was to go from one national park to the other; roughly it was down to Key West, head west then and do a bit of a circle around the interior states and down to Mexico. I was by myself on the motorcycle and it was set up with a little trailer on the back, packed with all my climbing gear, and basically I went from national park to national park.

A close friend of Ger's, John Cardozo, logged some of the early moments from Ger's American trip on his blog.

> Well dear Gerard's friends, the man, the legend, the stinking Irish has finally left the building … (Now I can say what I want about him!!) Yep, he is gone, bye bye, finito, hasta la vista … He left this morning, 2 May 1997, from Columbia, Maryland, and headed south. His first stop will probably be an Irish pub in Richmond, Virginia. I figure that's when he'll be needing refilling, Guinness refilling anyway. His first destination is the Great Smoky Mountains in North Carolina. As you all probably know, his final destination is Alaska.

Two more logs dated 5 and 6 May read as follows:

> I've just received a voicemail from Gerard at about 11.00 a.m. today from the Great Smoky Mountains. So obviously he made it to his first destination site. He said he is having a blast, or maybe he said he has a blister in his ass! I'm not sure, but in any case he said he saw a black bear 15 feet away, but he ran like hell … the bear, that is! I don't blame the poor bear, just look at what the Irish looks like now after four days' motorcycling without a shower!

Ger's First Encounter with Alaska

Again chance was to play a part in where Ger would end up next. He had decided to take in Alaska on his trip.

> What sparked the interest was a documentary on the National Geographic channel, a piece on the Kodiak brown bear. I thought to myself, wouldn't it be interesting if I could ride the motorcycle up there. I wasn't too sure what condition the roads were in, especially in northern Canada. Some people said 'don't be crazy, don't do it', but I did some investigating and the more I checked it out the more I wanted to do it. Oddly enough when I did get up there I ended up meeting one of the people that was actually in the documentary. We got chatting and they asked me what led me to Alaska and I told them the documentary, they couldn't believe it.

Ger McDonnell rolled into the beautiful state of Alaska on 10 July 1997; it was a day he would never forget as his sister Martha gave birth to a baby boy, Donnacadha, the same day. However, the beauty of Alaska presented a problem for Ger.

> Once I arrived in Alaska it was obvious to me I needed to spend more time there. Alaska is definitely a place of many extremes but those extremes are addictive. You can get super cold conditions and during the summer the interior can also get very hot. With those extremes comes extreme beauty as well. The harsh winters are not dark or dreary in the least, you have the northern lights and with the snow things are a lot brighter. I'll never forget when I was skating on this lake about a mile long and we were skating at night and the moon and northern lights were out and the reflection from both was on the ice; the ice had no snow, so it looked like still water. It was like we were skating in space. Sky above you and sky below you.

The climate suited his lifestyle and was better for his asthma than the damp Irish weather. On realising that he wanted to stay in Alaska, the next thing was to get a job, but first he had to call his boss and cancel his job in Norway.

> I guess one reason I decided to stay in Alaska and call my friend in Norway to refuse the job was Denali. Denali, which is the local name, means 'the high one', it is officially called Mount McKinley and is the highest mountain in North America. I wanted to climb it.
> It is an absolutely beautiful mountain even to look at. As the crow flies from Anchorage it's 150 miles [240km] away and you can see most of it on a clear day from Anchorage. It's permanently snow covered and stands proud at 20,320 feet [6,194m]. It amazes me every time I see it. Imagine it being in Dublin and on a clear day we can see it in all its glory from Limerick. It's roughly seven times the size of Corrán Tuathail and maybe twenty times colder.

Work was not as easy to come by in Alaska but Ger eventually met a man who led him to a possible job, followed by a very interesting interview.

> During the interview they say 'Oh we see by your résumé that you're Irish'; this is towards the end of the interview. The same fellow says that because you're Irish we're going to have to dock your wages a

certain amount each week and of course they all laughed. I laughed along and then I said, 'Oh you must be a Mormon company so.' It went down like a lead balloon really and I left that interview and was escorted to the door by one of them. Just as I was going out he tapped me on the shoulder and said, 'By the way, we *are* a Mormon company.' But they hired me.

He started work with Engineered Fire Systems, mainly in Anchorage but his work also brought him up to Prudhoe Bay in northern Alaska where he was put in charge of engineering and the drafting of demolition and construction packages. The year was a great one for Ger as he got back in touch with his climbing and photography; he started using the local mountains as a training ground for his attempt on Denali.

Ger the Musician

Anchorage also gave Ger a chance to get in touch with another passion: traditional Irish music.

> It's one of those cities too where it seems everybody knows everybody, there's a close community – climbing community and music community. In fact every Wednesday night there's a session of Irish Trad. There's not so many Irish people living there, just

Traditional Irish music session in Alaska. Ger is on the far right.

loads of Irish musicians – apart from me there's one other guy, John Walsh, who plays the banjo, I play the bodhrán in our band Last Night's Fun. We don't take ourselves that seriously; we play a few gigs and shows and there are also the festivals we play for. There is an Eskimo drum which we use from time to time; it's very basic and the rhythm is even more basic but it's great.

Ger's sister Stephanie remembers starting a band with Ger as children, 'We made our own instruments. I played and Ger sang and we recorded ourselves. I am convinced that it was those moments that led Ger to be in a band in Alaska and the name was ideal because any night Ger went out, he had fun.' His bodhrán skills were once described as someone putting a pair of runners into a drier and turning it on! Over the years, however, those skills were sought all over Alaska. The festivals allowed Ger to see even more of the Alaskan countryside and gain an understanding of the local tribes.

Alaska is beautiful but most parts are not very accessible. There's an old Alaskan saying that it's too big to experience in one lifetime, let alone one vacation. Certainly the native towns and villages are remote and it would be very expensive to get the bush flights out to these parts. The few times I have been out there our flights would have been paid for as part of the band. We have played Irish music to the Alaskan natives and of course they have loved it. There are many different tribes in Alaska – Inuit, Eskimo and Eyak just to name a few. Every year they all hook up in Anchorage for their annual meeting of the tribes. Most are successful business people and others actually live off the land. The Alaskan state gives the tribes money every year. Most receive large cheques for simply being part of a tribe. Tribes in Alaska are unique in the sense that they have a great handle on business. There's an amount of tribes in the lower 48s [the American states south of Alaska] that to this day are living in poverty.

Fellow bodhrán player and American band member Laura Hall picked up some good playing tips from Ger and enjoyed his sense of fun.

He gave his homemade double-ended brush to me, which was a bundle of thin wooden BBQ skewers bound tightly with silver duct tape. I have used it proudly ever since and when I play I think of his

Ger, pictured in 2006, with all his nieces and nephews. Back row *(l–r)*: Tracy Lynch, Aisling Holland, Sarah Lynch and Stephen Holland. Front row *(l–r)*: Donnacadha Lynch, Aoife Holland, Rebecca O'Brien, Emma O'Brien and Uncle Ger.

cheerful smile and bright eyes. I moved from Alaska in 2003 but I remember many fun times being silly with him at music festivals or on stage. Like one year John Walsh, our strictly trad bandleader, went on a trip to Ireland for the holidays. We had a Christmas céilí gig to do, so we planned to rock out, get a drummer and glitz it up. Gerard wore a kilt and big bulbous bunny boots like the North Slope workers wear in subzero weather. If anyone can make that outfit work for them, it would be him. We had the best time and everyone raved and cheered at our new Irish dance music.

A New Job and the Annual Homecoming

In 1998 Ger changed jobs and started working as an automation engineer for an oil company called Veco, which was heavily involved in the pipeline oil business in northern Alaska. It suited Ger perfectly as the work schedule involved two weeks on and two weeks off. While he was off he was able to enjoy both his music and climbing, working hard on both. That same year Ger landed in Dublin Airport for Christmas and came down by train to Limerick. To the astonishment of his brother J. J. who was there to meet him, he was holding deer antlers he had come across in Alaska. J. J. remembers the story well.

On 22 December 1998 I parked my car near Limerick station, where I was to collect my brother Ger who had got the train from Dublin to Limerick on his annual Christmas trip to spend the time with all of the family. As I crossed the road I noticed an individual weighed down with a large duffle bag in one hand and what appeared to be a medium-sized branch in the other. As I looked closer I smiled and thought to myself, who else could it be but Ger? I approached him with a certain inquisitiveness. As I got nearer, the branch transformed into an antler, and having greeted him he showed me his trophy. The antler was from an older Caribou stag that he had encountered while on a trek and he had got permission from the Parks and Wildlife Service to take it. The intricate nature of the individual wrapping of each of the pointed ends on the antlers with a cardboard structure was causing quite an amount of interest among the passers-by, which Ger really enjoyed. I enquired as to how the hell he even managed to get this on the train not to mind an aircraft, but he only laughed and said a few eyebrows were raised when he approached security and the check-in desk.

That Christmas Ger enthralled family and friends with tales of his new-found home in Alaska.

Ger always loved coming home so when it was time to go back to Alaska he went with a heavy heart. Going back this time his mind was occupied with getting into shape for Denali. Jeff Jessen and Mike Mays were going to attempt to climb this 6,194m/20,320ft mountain with him. Ger previously had only gone as high as 4,200m/14,000ft) and secretly he was worried as to how his body would react to the altitude.

4. THE START OF THE K2 ASCENT (AND DENALI SUMMIT AND RESCUE)

K2 was named in 1852 by a British surveyor taking observations from the south who observed two prominent peaks in the Karakoram range. K1 had a native name (Masherbrum), but K2 did not, so the shorthand name stuck.

The first recorded attempt to scale K2 was in 1902 when Oscar Eckenstein and the occultist Aleister Crowley attempted to scale K2 by the Northeastern Ridge. They reached 6,525m/21,407ft, and spent sixty-eight days on the mountain, of which only eight had clear weather. The next expedition, in 1909, was led by the Duke of Abruzzi, and reached a height of 6,250m/20,505ft via the southeast ridge above the Godwin Austen Glacier. The route was abandoned due to difficulty, with the Duke declaring that K2 would never be climbed. The first expedition to reach the summit, on 31 July 1954, was also Italian. It is interesting to note the closeness of their summit date to that of the 2008 expeditions – 1 August. Nobody has yet climbed K2 in the winter. The Abruzzi Route contains alternate sections of snow and rock, and offers some challenging rock climbs (known as technical climbs, as they involve complex use of ropes and other climbing equipment) on two famous features, 'House's Chimney' and the 'Black Pyramid'.

The Cesen Route, an alternative approach from the southeast, was named after Slovenian solo climber Tomo Cesen who successfully climbed K2 by this route in 1986. The Cesen Route is sometimes known as the Basque route because the Basque team that climbed K2 using this route in 1994 was the first team with a legal permit to do so. It would bring them along a spur

A view of K2 on the way to K2 Base Camp.

on the right side of K2's south face to the shoulder at 7,800m/25,600ft – there joining the standard Abruzzi spur route. Wilco had discussed the options with members of the Norit K2 Expedition, and all agreed that the Cesen route was the safer, if slightly more demanding, way to go. So this was the route on which they would pitch their four high-altitude camps. The Frenchman, Hugues d'Aubarède, an independent climber, had also chosen the Cesen Route. He had a small team that included his Pakistani climbing companion, Karim Meherban, and the American climber Nick Rice.

Both routes converge on the 'shoulder', which can be clearly identified in photographs of the mountain. From here there is only one main route to the summit, which involves scaling the narrow, almost vertical couloir known as the 'Bottleneck'. At the top of the Bottleneck climbers must continue to ascend beneath a huge serac, an ice formation which is inherently unstable and prone to sudden collapse (as ice and rock avalanches) as the glacier is in constant (albeit slow) motion.

29 May 2008, K2 Base Camp
After Ger and his fellow team of Norit climbers arrived at the K2 Base Camp, Ger complained about a lack of sleep on the trek to Base Camp in his first post from the camp site some days later.

Ta-daa … yeah we're here, K2 Base Camp. A bit behind the times here but sure that's the way it goes when solar charging chances are less than optimal for this little minimalistic solar set-up. All very uneventful to date apart from the breathtaking views of the Trango Towers, Masherbrum, GII, Broad Peak, etc and of course the one that we hope to befriend over the coming weeks. Last few days have been spent setting up base camp, sorting gear, food and catching up on sleep. The latter which we were denied en route by the nightly braying of a frustrated male donkey pleading with a mare more interested in the business of foraging. A common denominator there perhaps across the animal kingdom. Ha-ha! Laundry duties were also well overdue (low and all that the cleanliness standards we set ourselves on expeditions are). Some mild dust storms had mocked our efforts in that department. But no dust here – relatively speaking anyway. Pemba placed a call to his wife today to get the latest puja [a Buddhist devotional ceremony that has to

Ger recording preparations for the puja. (Courtesy Wilco van Rooijen)

be observed before setting foot on the mountain] date from his lama in Kathmandu. Looks like the Tibetan lunar calendar calls for 5 June between 8 a.m. and 10 a.m. as a good time. We also learned from Pemba that according to the Tibetan lunar calendar Saturday is never a good day to start anything significant ... hmm ... the Buddhist religion obviously wouldn't jive too well with Irish wedding schedules. Well, *tar éis an* Puja [after the Puja] we can start climbing in earnest. Until then we'll probably be shuttling gear to the depot at the base of the climb.

Ger also gave some hint as to the general good humour in the camp.

The kitchen staff has practical jokers amongst 'em. They placed a bar of soap next to a container of kerosene by the mess tent today and got a good laugh out of watching some of us fervently washing our hands with the stuff. Ha-ha! But we've practical jokers amongst us too ... But it's probably best not to pull too many fast ones on the lads that are preparing our food. Night now and one hears the glacier ache beneath and settle with the sound of distant gunshots at times. Stars galore and grand silhouettes surround. Tomorrow we build a puja altar and scout out a route to the base of the climb.

Ger, Pemba Gyalje, Jelle Staleman and Wilco van Rooijen in the mess tent at K2 Base Camp.

Ger finished his first post from K2 Base Camp with best wishes to his girlfriend, who was climbing Denali. 'Best of luck on Denali, Annie!'

They had arrived in the Base Camp for this most difficult of climbs, over 8,000m/26,000ft, on 29 May 2008. Nine years and four days earlier, on 25 May 1999, Ger and two of his friends, Jeff Jessen and Mike Mays, had set out to climb Denali – to make it his first climb over 6,000m/20,000ft. Ger recalled how the climb went in an interview with West Limerick 102 local radio.

> Finally getting to climb 'the high one', the day had arrived. On one of the first summit day attempts one of our members, Jeff, started to show signs of cerebral oedema [swelling of the brain caused by lack of oxygen] – which is similar to someone appearing drunk on the mountain, you lose your balance, your speech is slurred and generally you start talking gibberish. So we had no option but to bring him down to safety; if you descend just a few hundred feet you start to notice the difference in the patient. The condition is related to the pressure up there and of course the lower you go the less pressure. There's no exact explanation of what causes it.
>
> Peter Hackett is an American who is most experienced in the field. His theory is that it is related to drainage from the brain to the spine and he says that less air pressure in high altitude may create a blockage. The other dangerous condition is pulmonary oedema, which is fluid in the lungs, which again is caused by pressure. If you get any of these conditions and descend almost immediately you will be fine but you won't be going back up again. We had three team members on that trip. It was to be a life-changing trip for all of us. We were all roped together on at least 50m of rope and you'd have a coil at either end for rescue proposes. There could be 15m of rope between each climber and if someone did happen to fall through a crevasse it's easy to stop them from falling to their death. You'd be surprised at the friction on a lip of a crevasse. It's fairly high so it acts almost like a pulley and takes the load off you. The Denali ascent took almost four weeks – twenty-three days to the summit and a few days back down. As you're starting out on the mountain you leapfrog your way up with your provisions and gear. Essentially you actually end up climbing the mountain twice if not more. Also you need to acclimatise and especially on McKinley (Denali) you'd hang out at 4,300m/14,000ft for four to five days. People have stayed for four days but five is best, otherwise you're taking a

gamble. Once you have acclimatised it's then a matter of waiting for the weather to be in your favour. Often that can take a long time, especially on Denali as when the storms do come they tend to last for a while. If you are ascending and you get headaches then you're not fully acclimatised. When you're on the mountain with your snow goggles you are being protected from snow blindness. The day we ended up going to the summit a guy from another expedition removed his goggles as they were steaming up; he ended up with snow blindness and had to be rescued. Apparently it's excruciating pain – like having sandpaper rubbed in your eyes, that's how the feeling has been described to me. It's an extremely sore condition but it does wear off after six to eight days – with bad cases of it you just can't open your eyelids. He was lucky as he had partial vision in one eye so was able to move down the mountain.

The sense of achievement that I felt while on top of McKinley (Denali) was unbelievable. Even to this day I still rate the Alaskan range as the most beautiful in the world. It's just majestic – God's country, as we say. Just to be on it was a great achievement and in all these expeditions the most important thing I believe is to enjoy them and have a good time.

While Ger was on Mount McKinley (Denali), back in Kilcornan his old primary school was closely monitoring his progress. Ger was delighted with the interest the schoolchildren were showing and sent this email on his return.

The extent of the support from family, friends and parishioners was relayed back to me by my mother. The gesture of your pupils of Kilcornan national school at your most recent confirmation for instance was overwhelming [the pupils lit a candle for Ger on this occasion].

I'll fill you in on a little bit of the happenings on the mountain. I'll try not to bore you with details. So I'll bore you with a *Reader's Digest* version instead …

We arrive in Talkeetna early in the morning of 25 May with little or no sleep from packing the two days previous. Surprisingly we meet Brad and Barbara Washburn, both in their eighties. Barbara was the first woman to conquer Mount McKinley (Denali) in 1954; both Brad and Barbara had climbed it many times. They gave us oodles of useful hints in the last minutes before departing for the glacier. It seems that we're off to a great start and we can't believe that we had such good fortune to meet the Washburns. The flight in was beautiful, Base Camp was busy and the weather was fantastic. People were playing volleyball in their T-shirts and shorts at 2,200m/7,200ft …

Weather is great most of the way. We're feeling exceptionally fortunate to have had only a few days of travelling in whiteout conditions [when either snow, cloud or wind inhibit visibility].

Unfortunately Jeff and I develop chest infections from a flu we caught at Base Camp. But we get antibiotics from other climbers, rest regularly and climb slowly in the hopes of improvement. We start to ascend faster to 4,300m/14,200ft but sadly Jeff gets altitude sickness for the first time.

We rest and get Jeff looked after. The weather improves so we head for the summit. Jeff is our lead to the summit. The route is in good condition, no trail-breaking required so Jeff sets the pace to whatever he's comfortable with. We ascend slowly through a notoriously dangerous section of the mountain called the Denali Pass. We almost reach the top of the pass when we notice Jeff acting strange. We ask if he is OK. He tells us he is fine, just a slight headache. We reach the top of the pass at 5,500m/18,000ft and again confront Jeff about his condition.

He reassures us he's fine so we all continue to climb.

Unfortunately, at 5,895m/19,340ft our worst fears are realised when Jeff suddenly collapses to the ground. He tells us he is dizzy but needs time to recover. We wait a few moments, then perform some coherency tests; it's obvious to us now that he is suffering from HACE [high-altitude cerebral oedema]. We descend with him immediately. Eventually we arrive back to 5,250m/17,200ft high camp and begin to nurse Jeff back to health. He recovers quickly but realises he just can't risk another summit attempt.

We learn that some of the national park doctors are at this high camp, so they give him the once over and reassure us that it is safe for us to leave him and try our summit attempt for the second time.

Both Mike and I feel pretty weak from the day before and are not too sure if we have enough energy to make the summit. Knowing that climbers normally only make one summit attempt, we both agree that if we're feeling tired we turn around. Jeff helps us prepare while having mixed feelings about our second attempt.

Ger holds aloft the Milford Hospice sign. The hospice cares for terminally ill patients and their families, with some funding coming from the state and the rest from generous donations, such as the £15,000 raised by Ger, his family and friends.

Ger plays the bodhrán, given to him by his sister Denise, on the summit of Denali.

His fears are justified but we promise to concentrate on safety and not to be overcome by 'summit fever' [wanting to get to the top at all costs].

We set off and after a while we finally reach the summit ridge. With one step a vast expanse opens before me. The view is breathtaking and suddenly all tiredness seems to disappear, temporarily anyhow. Mike and I stand for a few moments and sort of laugh nervously at how narrow the ridge is to the summit. Climbers back in high camp had told us that in places you have just six inches of ridge to cross with a 1,200m/4,000ft drop to the south and an incredibly steep drop to the north. We climb ahead with extreme caution, placing protection at every rope's length, one foot in front of the other, like walking a tightrope.

Although dangerous, we can't but marvel at the beautiful surroundings. At 9.30 p.m. on 14 June, our twenty-first day on the mountain, both Mike and I stand on the highest mountain in North America – Mount McKinley. We're elated and for a laugh I celebrate by playing a little bodhrán that my sister Denise had sent me over from Ireland to play on the top. Mike looks at me as though I'm crazy but I'm too caught up in the moment to care. We phone our families; cheers and jubilation summarise the moment. The weather starts to change so we quickly prepare to descend. A mountain is never fully climbed until you are back down in the safety of high camp.

Jeff is waiting for our return and was about to initiate awareness of our situation amongst the park authorities before he spotted us through binoculars on the pass. We fall into our sleeping bags after eighteen hours of hard climbing; normally it takes just eight to ten hours. We've done it.

It takes us only two days to get back to Base Camp at 2,200m/7,200ft, where we wait with the other hordes of climbers for our flight out. We depart for Talkeetna on 28 June, our twenty-fifth day on the mountain. First order of the evening of course is a nice hot shower and the luxury of getting into fresh clothes. Then off to the restaurant/pub with our friends, where we party all night.

One bar in Talkeetna has a painting of Denali on the wall and the climbers that summit are encouraged to place their country's flag on it. It's a celebratory affair, where the attention is gathered from the entire crowd while the climbers place their flags on the summit.

The crowd erupts when they see the Irish flag being placed, the Americans because of their love for the Irish, the Europeans as they thought it was the Italian flag and everyone else as they had beers in them and it seemed like the right thing to do.

Mike Mays remembers the climb a little differently, with the ascent not going as smoothly as the pictures taken on the summit suggested.

As we arrived in Talkeetna, we brought forty days of supplies and fuel, and were quickly dubbed 'The Porky Pig Expedition' by Doug Geeting, our glacier pilot, because we had so much gear and fuel.

With Ger's big laugh and continuous smile, which only

complemented Jeff's and my constant big smiles and fun southern personalities, the Denali rangers quickly realised we intended not only to 'lay siege' to Denali but to have fun doing it every step of the way. We did not disappoint.

Jeff faltered high on the mountain and we had to lower him back to our camp at 5,250m/17,200ft, but Ger and I knew at Jeff's high point at about 5,915m/19,400ft that we could climb that big bad mountain if we just came back the next day.

After stabilising Jeff back at camp from a long day on the mountain spitting up blood and with broken ribs from coughing, Ger and I set about heading back up the mountain the following day at 11 a.m., with two guys from Idaho, three men from South Africa and two Taiwanese women following close behind us.

We soon outdistanced all the others and by 9.30 p.m. were alone, high on the summit ridge of Denali (6,127m/20,100ft), making our way across the narrow summit ridge to the true summit (6,194m/20,320ft).

We both climbed slowly onto the summit, smiling, whooping and hallooing in the clear bright Alaska daylight, and from there we both called home on the cell phone. We were on the highest point in North America, Ger's and my first summit over 6,000m/20,000ft!

It's really hard to describe the excitement surrounding such a moment. It's a feeling of accomplishment unlike any other in life, and both of us fought back tears of joy, of great pride in our accomplishment.

After our initial celebrations were over, I videotaped Ger playing the bodhrán on top of Denali – undoubtedly a first – and I planted an American flag in the snow in remembrance of my deceased father and younger brother. We then set about taking the traditional summit pictures. Aside from watching Ger play that bodhrán, what you don't know is the hilarious efforts it took to get those few summit pictures. Ger was climbing for Milford Hospice and he had carried a large sign for the summit. As Ger breaks the sign out of his pack, unrolls it and goes to hold it high above his head, the 30 mph [50km/h] gusting winds blow it out of his hands and it goes blowing off the northwestern part of the summit onto the snow about 30m/100ft down the mountain.

We look at each other, like: 'Okay, go get it!'

We agree that Ger will belay me down the mountain on the

climbing rope to get the sign, which we do successfully, and then we go about repeating the same picture, but once again he loses the sign as he holds it high and it goes blowing off the mountain in the same general direction. And again I am belayed down the mountain by Ger and get the sign and climb back up onto the summit. My third summit of Denali in less than thirty minutes!

Had the sign blown in any other direction than it did, it would have floated 2,400m/8,000ft off the vertical sides of Denali. God played a huge role in getting that sign in our pictures!

We then laughed and joked about having to break out the duct tape and tape the sign to Ger's hand, but on our third try we got the pictures. I doubt anyone in Alaska holds the distinction of such a funny scene on top of such a deadly mountain, and I can only think of one person who would laugh along with me at something like that happening – Ger. Of course, after that point, our descent became deadly serious when we ended up having to spend the next seventeen hours getting five fatigued and injured climbers back down to the 5,250m/17,200ft camp.

On Denali, Ger's good fortune in climbing partners was apparent when they became involved in the difficult descent that Mike Mays referred to. With the drama of taking their pictures and making the video of Ger playing the bodhrán on the summit of Denali, both men were there for about thirty minutes. Of the climbers they had overtaken earlier, the two Idaho men had turned back at 19,300ft, but the two Taiwanese women reached the summit while they were still there. The skies were now partly cloudy, having been mostly clear earlier, and the winds from the northeast had picked up to 30 mph (50km/h). Temperatures were also dropping rapidly from 10 °F (-12 °C) to -15 °F (-26 °C) on four inches of fresh snow. The climbers remained on the summit for another ten minutes before Ger and Mike started their descent, followed by the Taiwanese women. Halfway down the summit ridge the group met with the South Africans, who were still ascending. Mike and Ger told the South Africans they would leave their protection on the ridge (for their descent) and would wait for them at the football field where the rest of their survival gear was. By this time clouds had totally engulfed the summit and visibility had decreased to 150m/500ft.

On the way down the summit headwall Mike and Ger noticed that the older of the two Taiwanese women was beginning to have trouble descending. She appeared to be having difficulty with her balance and toppled from near the top of the summit headwall 4 to 6m/15 to 20ft before her partner arrested her fall. Her partner, surprisingly and without asking, tied a prusik (a friction hitch) onto Mike and Ger's rope and descended to her fallen partner. Communication was difficult as the Taiwanese spoke very little English. The group continued to descend, with the Taiwanese in front. The Taiwanese fell several times again before they reached the football field. On arriving at the field Mike and Ger watched the Taiwanese women obviously struggling. They tried to communicate with them but were never convinced that everything was okay. One of the women collapsed while the other tried to keep her warm, feed her, and encourage her to keep moving. Finally, the women told Mike and Ger that they would stay at the football field and descend the next morning but that they did not have any bivouac gear. Mike and Ger convinced them that they would not survive the night without proper equipment. Shortly thereafter, the South Africans arrived. The group now agreed to descend together, with the Taiwanese women in the middle. They descended extremely slowly. The weak Taiwanese woman was stumbling and fell several times. Visibility had decreased to 30m/100ft and the wind was a steady 65km/h/40 mph. They could hear the wind howling below at Denali Pass. The group then attempted to descend the easier slope to the right of the wind meter rocks.

While descending, Mike punched through a crevasse and had to climb out. The lead South African fell into the same crevasse before his team finally arrested his fall. Everyone regrouped above and tried to communicate but failed due to weather conditions. Mike and Ger found out later that one of the South Africans had become snow blind and was having a difficult time maintaining his balance. The group slowly descended to Denali Pass.

Once at the pass the Taiwanese women once again decided to bivvy and carve out a seat in the snow, but were again urged to continue the descent. Mike and Ger gathered everyone's pickets and began to set up a running belay every 21m/70ft to keep each rope team on at least two anchors. The descent from the pass was slow, taking five and a half hours, as the group rarely used the trail due to poor visibility. The Taiwanese and South Africans experienced several falls, forcing Mike and Ger to shorten the anchors to 12m/40ft. The group reached the 5,250m/17,200ft camp at 7 a.m., eighteen hours after departing.

At the camp the following day, a ranger interviewed all individuals involved. The Taiwanese and South Africans were extremely thankful for Mike and Ger's help. The snow-blind South African was treated in the field and short-roped down the following day to 4,300m/14,000ft and treated again. The Taiwanese women spent the entire next day in their tent and safely descended the day after.

A young Ger in Alaska practising with his snow shoes.

Mike and Ger were humbled by the experience but stated several times that there was no way they could have left any of the other climbers; they were thankful they all made it down unscathed. Both were awarded the Denali Pro Pin by the Denali National Park Rangers with the following citation:

Mike Mays and Gerard McDonnell are excellent examples of Denali

National Park's rescue policy and acted as if rehearsed directly from our booklet and orientation. Their entire expedition descended from a high elevation (5,900m/19,300ft) because one member was ill demonstrating sound thinking in avoiding accidents and rescues. Mike and Gerard knew there was an NPS patrol at 5,250m/17,200ft but chose to act as members of the 'international climbing community' and take on a huge responsibility rather than just pass on the information. Many climbers would have (and historically, have) made a different decision when faced with the same dilemma as Mike and Gerard. The Organization were convinced the decisions and actions made by these two climbers avoided at least a costly and time consuming rescue and probably a few grimy statistics.

Mike and Ger later wrote a letter to the Mountain Rescue, in which they stated:

Both of us have a renewed respect for the job the NPS Rangers are faced with on Denali. We were also both pleased to learn of the Denali Pro Pins in that it is an excellent way to foster good relations and cooperation, not only among fellow climbers, but between the individual climbers and NPS Rangers as well.

Mike and Ger were tested to the limits on Denali, but that experience allowed Ger, for the first time, to show the kind of man he was.

5. WAITING ON K2 (AND FROM DENALI TO EVEREST)

K2, 5 June 2008

Base Camp on K2 was at 4,954m/16,000ft, and Ger, along with his team members, spent a number of days setting up camp, preparing for the next stage of the climb and just acclimatising.

Ger leading a singsong at K2 Base Camp.

Securing the tents to the slopes of K2. (Courtesy Wilco van Rooijen)

On 5 June, at around 8 a.m., the Norit team held a puja ceremony led by Ger's friend Pemba, an ethnic sherpa from Nepal who practised a form of Tibetan Buddhism, as the sherpas had their roots in Tibet. Pemba would not start his climb before this important ceremony had taken place. From his blog post a few days later Ger recounted the detail.

> Pemba had spoken with a lama before the expedition who blessed the prayer flags and coached him on the procedure. He provided recordings of lama chants to play on his mp3 player during the ceremony, and to great effect. The atmosphere was such that the sounds seemed to emanate from the puja altar itself rather than from the little mp3 player. Sharing the top of the flagpole are an Irish flag, compliments of Annie, Norit K2 flag and a Pakistan flag. The latter was sneakily placed on the top of the flagpole by one of the kitchen staff while we were sleeping. A vie for the top spot. But Pemba put a stop to all that and put all the flags in the top spot … so much so that it's hard to see the Pakistan flag.

Climbing and ferrying loads on the lower slopes of K2. Ger (in foreground in bottom photo) is carrying a pack with additional ropes. (Courtesy Wilco van Rooijen)

After the ceremony Ger, along with Pemba and some other members of the Norit team, including Sheeny, made the trip to Camp 1 – first to help with acclimatisation and then the next day to bring up equipment. The same system of gradual acclimitasation that Ger had described on Mount McKinley (Denali) would be used to accustom the climbers to the far greater altitude on K2. The principle adopted by Wilco was the tried-and-tested one of climbing to a higher altitude during the day, and returning to a lower one to sleep at night. This allowed the body to recuperate from the effects of the loss of oxygen before going up into thin air again. At the same time, in the course of each climb, necessary gear for the high camps including ropes, ice screws, tents, food and cooking equipment was carried up the mountain in relay. It takes several weeks to acclimatise and to set up the four camps needed before attempting the summit of an 8,000m+ mountain. As the oxygen supply reduces, the climbers move more slowly and the equipment weighs more heavily. Rest days are needed between sorties, so nothing happens quickly.

The concept of 'camp' at high altitude is extremely basic: shelter, in the form of a small, usually two-person, tent, pegged down on whatever level ground can be found: sometimes a rock base would have to be improvised to compensate for the angle of the slope. Inside the tent would be cooking equipment and food, mainly dehydrated, and sleeping bags. Water was obtained by melting snow. The camp was basically a place to shelter and refuel, while concentrating on the task of climbing higher up the mountain.

Ger had been surprised to discover that the Norit expedition was the only one in the K2 Base Camp so far that year. 'We're still very strangely the only team here. To have this particular mountain all to ourselves since 29 May is a thrill – although it'll be a short-lived one. The hordes are surely around the corner.'

The next day Ger and his team would take a rest before climbing back up to Camp 1 where they were almost finished attaching the fixed lines to Camp 2. Once that was done they would start shuttling equipment to Camp 3, and finally Camp 4, from where they would eventually make their assault on the summit.

While they were the only team in the K2 Base Camp, Ger noted that they were not the only guests to have made it from Askole – and the kitchen porters were none too happy.

And there's a mouse in the house! And Sheeny turns out to be quite the mouse whisperer. He managed a little pet once or twice. This act however has turned against him somewhat as some of the team members reckon they've a 'special' relationship. It was called Fred initially but Fred looks very pregnant, much to the kitchen staff's chagrin. Fred's increasingly evident pregnancy has caused an increased need for a name change. 'Sheena' has stuck, much to Sheeny's delight. At 5,000m/16,400ft we're not too sure whether to admire its ability to survive this altitude year round or to sympathise with the poor misfortunate for its decision to hop into an Askole crate and inadvertently relocate. She's a welcome friend to the climbing team but the kitchen staff look very confused at the team lighting up at her appearance. We suspect a mysterious disappearance in the not too distant future.

As always, Ger literally kept the Irish flag flying, with some concession to the other nationalities in the K2 Base Camp.

An Irish flag, handmade by a tailor in Skardu, flaps outside the tent representing the small Irish contingent of the Norit K2 team. In truth though, it acts more as a welcome beacon to any Irish person who should wander into camp. Curiously, none of the other members brought along their country's flag. So just to keep the Dutch lads appeased the Irish flag is wrapped around the flagpole from time to time such that only the orange flies. More especially for their Dutch–Italian European cup match this Monday.

Acclimatisation on K2 left plenty of time to think, read and, for Ger, to socialise both with his team members and the Pakistani staff who manned the kitchen. Ger had a great relationship with the porters and staff who supported him on his climbs. He had got to know the sherpas while climbing Everest in 2003, and made a firm friend of Pemba Gyalje. Here he was first introduced to HAPs. These were Pakistanis from the surrounding area, who had been born at high altitude, and therefore, like the sherpas, had a certain level of natural acclimatisation to living at height. But they did not have the sherpas' long tradition of mountain guiding, and many climbers considered the HAPs a poor alternative to a sherpa. For the HAPs, it was a prestigious job (albeit not without its dangers, including altitude sickness) with good pay and excellent perks – the climbers often donated some of their expensive clothing to their helpers on leaving, for example. Ger recognised that one of the young Pakistani HAPs was inexperienced on the mountain and showed him how to use the ropes to assist him. The porter was amazed that a mountaineer would take the time and effort to demonstrate these skills to him. Ger's first experience of working with porters had come some years earlier when he had the help of sherpas. Ger was not used to anyone else carrying his gear or helping him on the mountain. If anything, he delighted in helping others, which was not always a good idea as the porters firmly saw this as their area of expertise. On a previous climb Ger had fallen foul of a sherpa when he tried to tie a fellow climber's bootlace that had come undone.

> There was a funny incident – I thought it was funny anyhow – en route where Hannah's bootlace became untied and I was approaching her. I bent down to tie it for her, but as I was doing that I got a whack on the backside from a porter telling me to move on. I laughed at him and continued to tie the lace. Suddenly I received a second, stronger whack on the backside and he again told me to stop doing what I was doing and move on. I was doing his job and he was serious. The smallest little chore they regarded as their job and that was that. They're extraordinary people and climbers. Thankfully the Irish sense of humour fitted in perfectly with the Nepalese; we both enjoyed each other's company.

Everest in View and Last Night's Fun

Having completed his first climb over 6,000m/20,000ft in 1999 Ger was, for the first time, thinking of attempting a climb that would require the expertise of sherpas and high-altitude porters. Having reached the summit of Denali, he was now drawn to the world's tallest mountain, Mount Everest. 'After the success on Denali, I started reading about Everest – I read that a lot of people climb Denali as a pre-Everest climb. Slowly my target was set about climbing Everest, so I trained and researched what the climb was all about.'

First Ger went back to work and then home to Ireland for his Christmas trip. This was an annual pilgrimage for Ger, an opportunity to meet his mother and all the family. The second part of this trip was to Dublin to meet his old college friends, with whom he had a special bond. In 2000, Ger's contract with the oil company, Veco, where he had enjoyed the two-weeks-on/two-weeks-off work schedule, finished but he was lucky enough to get another job almost immediately, this time working as a systems analyst with a company called Glacier Software Inc. in Anchorage. They did a lot of work up in Prudhoe Bay and Deadhorse. Again this work suited Ger's lifestyle, two weeks on and two weeks off, so there was plenty of time for climbing and playing music.

At this point Ger had successfully joined one of Alaska's premier trad bands, Last Night's Fun, led by the talented Irishman John Walsh. John and Ger were great friends and always had *craic* (the Irish word for 'fun') together. In 2002 the band was playing at a St Patrick's Day céilí and concert in Anchorage. Mark Ward, the fiddle player, had recently become a father of an adorable baby girl named Piper. Mark's wife, Dana, showed up unexpectedly at the céilí so they all could see the new arrival. Everybody fussed over Piper, including Ger. Later that night when Dana was undressing Piper for bed she found a handwritten note in the pocket of the baby's jumper: 'Piper, call me when you're thirty.' It was signed 'Gerard'. The following week at another performance Ger found a note one of the band had slipped into *his* pocket. Having read it he pushed his chair back from the table and burst into laughter, that broad Ger smile gleaming at everyone. The note read, 'Hi Gerard, thanks for your note. Well, I'll have to think about it. If I call you when I'm thirty, you'll be, what, in your sixties? Your teeth will probably be all black, and you could be pooping in your pants – just like I am now. Piper.'

That same summer Ger's brother J. J., along with their cousin Mike McDonnell and friend John Coleman, visited him in Anchorage and went on to have an adventure-packed holiday travelling around with Ger. J. J. recalls one particular story.

> John Coleman, Mike and I travelled to Anchorage in July 2000 where we were met by an enthusiastic Ger and his girlfriend Tracy. John Hanly [a cousin and one of Ger's closest friends] had travelled the week before from Washington and had hiked and climbed with Ger for the week.
>
> The following morning we got our gear together for a four-day trip and Ger informed us that it was so remote that $30 would be more than enough to take with us. We flew on three different types of aircraft and ended up in the secluded national park called Katmai. In Katmai we camped at a site adjacent to the lake where the river planes landed and took off, ferrying passengers to this remote park.
>
> The next day we walked up to the falls to view the brown bears feeding on the salmon that were returning upstream to spawn. The following day we were ferried by bus to a lookout point 30 miles from the cabins and the camp site, from where we hiked into the sandy valley below.
>
> It was a phenomenal experience – with the exception of our diet during the day which had been specifically prepared by Ger

Last Night's Fun *(l–r)*: John Walsh, Kenny Karabelnikoff, Dan Possumato, Ger and Mark Ward.

to keep up our energy. Mike took such a dislike to the trail mix that even when I mention the trip to this very day it's the first thought that comes into his head. At night we had a cooked meal using hydrated food and iodine mixed through the ice. On 31 July we celebrated my birthday at 11.30 p.m. as the sun was setting – a special meal of hydrated potatoes, one of my favourite foods. On our trek out to the collection point to get the bus, the rangers reckoned we had the luck of the Irish as, unknown to us, there was a sandstorm building up behind and we made it all the way to the bus before it hit. The sandstorm was so bad that the river planes were grounded that night at the camp site and were only able to fly again the following morning.

On our return journey to the camp site we were all salivating as Ger had informed us that there was an 'all you can eat' buffet. However, perhaps we had looked forward to it too much because, by the time we showered and were ready to go, I announced that I wasn't feeling great and the others said likewise. However, when the scent of the food-filled bains-marie filled our nostrils we focused on the job at hand. We paid our $15 and proceeded to fill our plates. This exercise was repeated five times, at which point the waitress told us that the chef had actually come out to see for himself that there were only five Irish guys consuming all this food … I told the waitress to inform the chef it was a good job we weren't feeling that well!

As we finished our desserts Ger made his way up to the small bar and enquired if there was enough beer for five thirsty Irish guys and the response was positive. We pooled the remainder of our money and began to drink. We continued to drink until the money ran out, at which point we were joined by the waitress and other staff who had just finished their shift. As the night progressed we established that one of the waitresses from Canada had lived with a folk singer in Belfast in Northern Ireland, so she began to sing. Ger was an avid singer and the rest of us gave it our best shot. We had an absolutely incredible evening. The following morning the head ranger did not greet us with the same chirpy Hollywood-Irish greeting of 'top of the morning to you' but scowled instead. John Hanly had departed on the first plane out and later informed Ger why the ranger had been so cool. John said that when he went to the plane there were two cabins of people checking out as they had failed to sleep due to the singing. The head ranger was very upset as this had not happened since the camp was set up some thirty years previously.

The remainder of the holiday was also incredible. Ger had arranged whale-watching trips and visits to national parks to view the splendour of the wildlife and scenery. This culminated with a barbecue on the night of 10 August, the eve of our departure. According to Ger, he was just having a few friends around. Before the party started he asked me if I would do him a favour, and after all he had done for us I couldn't refuse. Ger was working for Veco at the time and had told me that his boss wanted to treat a client of theirs who would be staying in the Alyeska resort, a five-star hotel south of Anchorage which we had visited during the week. Ger said all I had to do was bring an envelope of money to this man. I asked why the man didn't simply come to Anchorage to collect the money but Ger said that he had to work the following morning and that his boss had asked him to do this favour.

As we returned from Denali National Park we called into a local store and got some food for the barbecue. Ger's housemates had already got the show on the road, and I couldn't believe the amount of rib-eye, salmon, caribou, moose and food that was laid on. Soon Ger's friends arrived laden with desserts, salads and various beers and wines. Then to my surprise a birthday cake was produced and I enquired whose birthday it was only to be told it was mine! Ger had arranged this incredible party for my birthday. It was another night that I will cherish for the rest of my life. Just before I retired to bed Gerard asked if I was still okay to do this thing for him in the morning. I confirmed that I was.

Just three hours after I had climbed into the rucksack Ger was leaning over me calling my name. My body was only waking limb by limb, so Ger pressed me to hurry up. I was putting on a pair of shorts and a T-shirt but Ger suggested I wear something warmer. Ger gave me a coat and put a cup of coffee in my hand. Having gathered the keys and the envelope I went out to the jeep, where I was stunned to find Mike and John Coleman ready to go. Just as we were departing Ger informed me that when I got to Alyeska resort I was to go to reception and give my name and they would direct me where to go. Ger jumped on his dirty bike and headed off to work and I drove off as quickly as possible, wondering what on earth was going on.

Arriving in the resort car park I woke John and Mike and told them that I would only be a few minutes. I gave my name at reception and the receptionist said they were expecting me. Instead of asking me for the envelope, she gave me a ticket and told me to proceed to the sky lift area and to take the cable car to the hill top. So now the client wasn't even going to come down to the hotel to meet me. I felt like turning around but I was there at that stage and I would do it for Ger. On presenting my ticket the sky lift operator said, 'Oh Mr McDonnell, we have been expecting you.' At this stage I was getting quite concerned. Was this 'client' with the Mafia or some underground crime boss, I wondered. We headed up in the sky lift and although the scenery was spectacular, in my anxious state I could not appreciate it. As we neared the top I noticed two people paragliding above the cable car. At the top the operator asked that I wait on the platform and that a gentleman would meet me as soon as possible.

The wait on the platform then began. The cable car continued up and down numerous times with people getting in and out, but no one approached me. All I got was a smile from the operator. As the time passed my suspicions were growing. What the hell was going on and who was this mystery client?

The sky lift approached with the operator and one passenger. The door opened, and a man with what appeared to be a large backpack stepped out. As I moved to get on the man said, 'You're J. J.? I believe you have something for me.' At this point I thought it strange that I hadn't been given a password or a secret handshake. I gave the man the envelope and I went to board the lift he said, 'Come with me.' What does he want to do, count the money? I follow him to the hilltop restaurant, outside which we sit on a bench. He then produces a sat phone and dials a number. He hands it to me and says, 'It's for you.' I take the phone and nervously say hello. The voice at the other end is Ger's, who shouts 'happy birthday' and tells me I'm about to go paragliding. What I experienced at that point was a mixture of shock and relief. Now when I recall this story I get a lump in my throat and my eyes well up as I think of the excitement in Ger's voice and the trouble he had gone to in arranging this surprise.

The warm clothes made sense now but one thing still puzzled me: how did Ger manage to get John and Mike up without telling them anything? So the paraglide instructor suited me up and put me in a harness. He explained how I was to run off the top of the plateau and not slow down when the pressure came on. He shouted 'one, two, three, go' and suddenly we were airborne, half a mile over this magnificent scenery. The adrenaline flowed quickly and I really cherished the moment. The instructor asked if I was okay with him performing some spirals. I replied yes, not really having had time to think. It was the most exhilarating experience of my life, and minutes later, to my great disappointment, the instructor said that when I hit the ground I was to bend my knees and start running again. I was awestruck by the entire experience and when the instructor pulled his chute together I told him my story. He laughed. Suddenly his phone rang, and after a brief conversation he told me we'd got the session in just in time. Apparently the mountain was now closed as the US army was setting off avalanche charges that failed to detonate during the winter.

I returned to the jeep to find the two asleep. As I recounted my story, they replied that they knew everything. Ger had sworn them to secrecy but they went along to video my paraglide. So now the final mystery was solved. We returned to Anchorage and, before we began packing, decided to watch the video. I noted, however, that there were two paragliders in the sky, and after some investigation it transpires that the lads had recorded the wrong jump. So whoever did a tandem paraglide on 11 August 2000 at approx. 10.15 a.m., I have the video! We packed our bags and Ger returned from work to drop us to the airport. During the entire journey there was a roguish smile on his face. He had well and truly got me.

In 2001 Ger and close friend Karen Herzenberg flew to the Talkeetna mountain range to climb the Sultana Route on Mount Foraker on 15 May. Again, what was supposed to be just a few days ended up being close to twelve. Most expeditions need a name for their check-in and this team's name was the Effen Pansies. Typical Ger humour.

The two were travelling with snowshoes and a CB radio as well as their other climbing gear. They lost a tent which was buried in a snowstorm and experienced some of the worst storms in a long time on that expedition. For some days they were stranded in their tent due to heavy snow and Karen suffered frostbite blisters on four fingers. Unfortunately, due to the small weather window, the pair could not get to the summit and only managed to reach an elevation of 3,800m/12,500ft. They flew out of Talkeetna on 27 May.

In 2002, J. J. and his mother Gertie travelled to Alaska to visit Ger who had always wanted to show his mother the beauty and hidden treasures the state had to offer. He brought the pair in his jeep across as much of Alaska as he could possibly manage within the time available. It is a trip that Gertie will never forget. Later that year Ger came home for a few weeks and went to Scotland to get in some ice climbing on Ben Nevis.

All this time Ger was thinking about climbing Mount Everest but it was a chance meeting on a trip home in 2003 that brought the dream closer to reality. 'I had a friend in Ireland, Liadain, who was also a mutual friend of Irish adventurer Pat Falvey. She knew I was interested in climbing Everest, and she told Pat about me.'

Pat Falvey was planning a trip at that time and agreed to meet this young man who was determined to climb Everest. He clearly remembers his first meeting with Ger and the impression he made.

I have had many great experiences in my expedition life as an adventurer, but one of the greatest was meeting Ger McDonnell in early 2003. When we met, there was an immediate energy radiating between us.

He had a glint in his eye, a childish grin on his face, and when he spoke, he did so with a vibrant passion about his love of mountains and family – a great combination. I immediately connected to him as a person of integrity.

Within minutes, I knew this friendship would grow. I hadn't seen this enthusiasm in anyone I had met in years. He visited me at The Mountain Lodge [Falvey's home and work base in Kerry] in the hope of convincing me that we needed someone like him on the expedition to Mount Everest, and his conviction made an big impact. His no-nonsense approach and self-belief captured my attention and affection immediately.

Ger walked in, introduced himself and got to the point.

'I know you're going to Mount Everest and I would love to join you. I believe I would make a great team player; I'm strong and I know I can reach the summit.'

He paused for a second and to reinforce his point, continued, 'I've done lots of stuff in Alaska; I know I'm a good climber, I'm strong and I want to do it.'

He went on to tell me he had dreamed about big mountains for most of his life and he wanted to climb Everest. He had a belief in his convictions. I remember smiling to myself at the time, laughing at the idea that Ger had a dream and nothing was going to stop him. I remembered feeling that way myself once.

I knew that this guy sitting in front of me, from Limerick – right up the road – believed he could climb Everest and from that first meeting I believed he would. Within minutes he had convinced me that not only was he a good climber but also showed all the traits of being a good teammate … and before he left that day I had decided to add Ger to the team. I also knew that the person that stood in front of me had the potential to do far greater adventures than I had ever conceived of myself. I knew even then that he had the potential of being a far greater mountaineer than I.

Over the coming months I got to know Ger better. He was not only a good climber, but he loved Ireland with a passion. Ger became the life and soul of our group no matter where we went.

So impressed was Pat with Ger that he decided to invite him on his next trip that very year, but this presented a problem for Ger.

Sure enough, one day Pat phoned me up and invited me onto the Irish team. Unfortunately I was financially committed to another expedition to go and climb in Antarctica. I had intended to climb Everest in 2004–5 but not in 2003. When he called me and I had to turn him down I had rather mixed feelings about missing out on the chance to climb with an all-Irish team on Everest, but by the same token I was excited about the prospect of climbing in Antarctica, especially Mount Tyree, at 4,852m [15,919ft] the second highest mountain of Antarctica.

A few weeks had passed and a friend of mine and one of the leaders in this expedition called me and said we had to cancel our trip. I was disappointed but straight away wondered if Pat still had any places left on his expedition. I phoned him and told him my story – I asked if there were any spaces left and he said there were and that I was in … so that's how I ended up on the 2003 Irish Everest Expedition.

Of course I was in Anchorage and the rest of the team were in Ireland. I guess Pat was checking me out but I had never met the others and the idea of climbing a monster like Everest and without knowing your team was a concern for me but it turned out to be great and we all got on fantastically. I finally met the team at Dublin Airport before we left.

Having got the good news from Pat, I phoned my mother. I wasn't sure how she'd react but thankfully she didn't sound too concerned. 'Any chance you'd help me raise some money?' I asked, and we both laughed. I was serious, though.

As ever the parish of Kilcornan and those surrounding were brilliant; a dance and a raffle were organised. An amount of money was raised, but three quarters of it came from my own pocket. The huge cost of climbing a mountain like Everest is the permit to the local government. That's where the big money goes, with the rest to a facilitating company in Kathmandu that provides sherpas, porters, food and cooks. Today the cheapest trek to Everest would cost about €22,000.

The sherpas are paid well and are very proud of their jobs; indeed one of the best jobs in Nepal as a sherpa is to climb Everest and the surrounding peaks.

So in 2003, as the Irish Everest Expedition was getting ready to depart from Dublin Airport, a very strong supporting group travelled from all parts of the country to wish them well. The families gathered in the lounge and children ran around excitedly as Hannah Shields introduced them to Freddie T. Bear. Freddie the teddy bear was the brainchild of Pat Falvey and Clare O'Leary as an educational exercise for schoolchildren to follow their adventures online. Pictures were taken, and then finally the time had come for Ger to begin the journey of a lifetime.

6. NEW ARRIVALS ON K2 (AND RECALLING THE EVEREST SUMMIT)

K2, 9 June 2008

At Base Camp on K2, the task of fixing lines to Camp 4, from where the team would launch their attempt on the summit, was interrupted by a European Championship soccer match between Holland and Italy on Monday 9 June. The Dutch members of the team decided to sweat it out in their orange down suits and the Irish flag that hung outside the Norit tent was flying in Dutch mode, showing orange only. Happily for the Dutch members – Wilco, Cas, Jelle and Roeland – Holland won 3–0. The match was only a brief distraction, however, from the serious business of climbing, and progress was continuing steadily towards achieving their goal, as recorded by Ger in his log on 9 June 2008:

> We've fixed up to 200m above Camp 2 and are staging further fixing progress après Camp 2 set-up. Hope to be back up the mountain fixing to Camp 3 on 12th and 13th. Interesting and enjoyable climbing thus far, with plenty of route variance. Spectacular views and more enjoyable than the Abruzzi thus far. The Basque/Cesen route lacks the illusion of climbing through an asteroid belt of falling stones for one. That's not to say that this route isn't without the danger of falling rocks. The amount of rock fall witnessed thus far has been few and far between. Weather forecast seems to be complying with our plans. The last few nights the base camp glacier has been very active. Certainly the glacier seems more active than any of us remember. We've felt several shockwaves both during the day and at night. All harmless. One crack almost sounded like the

birth of a nearby crevasse. Interesting to be able to feel the glacier move beneath us so frequently.

Regarding the climb: some of the lads are making a run up tomorrow to set up Camp 2. We'll head up the following day to fix lines further towards Camp 3. Weather has been great. Nights spectacular with a waxing moon.

Progress continued steadily, but after five days Base Camp was a busier place with the arrival of more international teams. Ger had seen this as inevitable. 'We have our first neighbours here in Base Camp – a French team. They promptly stopped in for a cup of tea and a chat and filled us in on some of the international news. On the mountain the lads – Wilco, Roland, Mark and Jelle – headed up towards Camp 2 today. Court to Camp 1. Tomorrow morning the Camp 2 bunch return to Base Camp while Cas, Pemba, Court and myself head up to Camp 2. Pemba, Cas and I then hope to continue fixing lines to Camp 3 and plan to return Saturday morning as the weather is forecasted to deteriorate somewhat on Sunday.'

The dangers on the mountain were not to be underestimated, as a post from Mark Sheen, the team's Australian member, a day later, makes clear.

It has really been a step by step, getting used to the mountain for me, especially going past Camp 1 towards Camp 2 which includes a mixed traverse, which for me by myself and the first time was a little scary especially when I was narrowly missed by a rock which I only saw as it passed. This was probably due to climbers above and/or being there in the heat of the midday sun. After a few days' rest, on 11 June I went to Camp 2 direct with my pack full volume wise and fairly heavy with Wilco, Jelle and Roeland and managed to complete the traverse to Camp 2 with relative calm, with me arriving at Camp 2 in the afternoon. Camp 2 is an 'airy' camp perched close to a large rock buttress on a dugout snow ledge with two tents, access of the farther tent having to be passed on the rock side of the first tent. It also has a very interesting small rock ledge for a toilet which requires care. After reaching Camp 2 and sharing with Wilco in the furthest tent he kindly gave me a cup of soup and then after another one, some salami and a freeze-dried meal, and after some chatting settled for sleep – or trying to sleep. The night for me wasn't that good, with a bumpy ridge resulting in some tossing and turning. I also by early morning didn't feel that

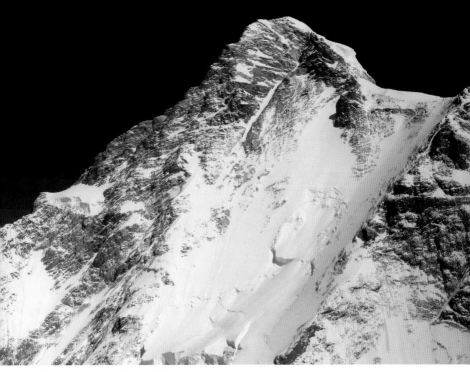

A view of the upper west face of K2.

well and by 6 a.m. was sick once in a bag. I never seem to react that well to freeze-dried meals, especially at camps on the mountains. Anyhow, our group decided to go down at 7 a.m. on the 12th so that we could let the other team of Ger, Pemba, Cas and Court come up without any fear of rocks being kicked down. I left Camp 2 at just after 7 a.m. not feeling too well, mainly just lack of energy, probably being due to the hour before and not having much in my system. Wilco had already left camp about ten minutes before. I proceeded cautiously down with Jelle and Roeland not too far behind and eventually made it to the traverse which I went along cautiously but surprisingly more confident. Eventually I made it down to Base Camp cautiously, but with my own power, at 11 a.m. so all was well. Now after a few days' recovery we plan to go up on the 17th, everything permitting, and sleep at Camp 2 and then Camp 3 which will hopefully be established by the rest of the team who leave tomorrow morning. So with a big South Korean team arriving today our team is making great progress.

The next day Ger gave a further update from K2.

We've almost fixed the lines to Camp 3. Looks like the home straight into that camp should be more like walking up a gradual snow slope than the prior mixed, and interesting, climbing that the route has presented thus far. More of that for later of course above Camp 3. The question of what altitude the fixed lines end at, at the moment, seems difficult to answer. With all the 'devices' (as Pemba calls them), more accurate altitude guesstimates probably come from a bit of intuition and some fantastic beta pictures [high resolution format photographs] with great supporting commentary, received pre-expedition from Fabrizio. Based on this it seems logical, to some of us that might be wishing to be higher than we actually are, that the lines end around 6,900m [22,700ft]. But that's all hogwash sort of postulating anyway. Bottom line – we're almost to Camp 3. Wilco, Cas, Roeland and Jelle have ascended this morning to Camp 2.

A lot of movement then planned for the mountain tomorrow. Wilco and Jelle will finish the fixing to Camp 3 while Cas and Roeland follow a little later with provisions to set up the camp. Sheeny, Court, Pemba and I will ascend to Camp 2. We'll then exchange teams at Camp 3 – ourselves moving up with further provisions for Camp 3 and beyond and the first group, Wilco etc., will descend to Base Camp. The following day then Pemba and I hope to spend the day reviewing the route above 3 to Camp 4, with the hope of fixing as much as possible.

A little problem we've run into now though is that we're running short of fixed line. Once the shortage raised its ugly head more was ordered from Skardu. From early on one important, and expensive, roll of 200m 5mm Spectra [cord] went mysteriously missing somewhere between Islamabad and Skardu. Probably hidden accidently under a seat of one of the many broken-down minibuses en route. We were hoping we could do without but when we alerted our local facilitating company, Jasmine Tours, of the lack of fixed line they went well out of their way to solve the problem. They promised a delivery within four days via an athletic Askole porter. We're not too sure how much this Skardu rope will weigh but that porter will end up carrying 500m of 7mm some 85km [53 miles] in four days. Very impressive stuff and a substantial tip will go his direction. A timely arrival could be instrumental. But with what we have to work with at the moment – three 200m rolls of 5mm and four dynamic ropes. Two of those 5mm rolls are for summit day. So they're not to be touched. Which leaves us with one roll of 5mm and the dynamic ropes to work with. We hope to be able to salvage some previously existing fixed line. Weather permitting and if we're lucky with the state of previous fixed line we hope to have fixed 70 per cent to Camp 4 on our next jaunt up the hill.

Of course here we are talking schedules, benchmarks, etc and it's raining now in Base Camp and who knows how that will affect things up the mountain. In fairness though, we were well due some bad weather as to date it's been uncharacteristically photogenic. But even at that, this spell isn't anything dramatically bad. Far from it. Some lazy drops, more like. The precipitation could certainly be for the better though as the route could do with a sprinkling of snow here and there. Radio call with the lads at Camp 2 at 6 p.m. and we'll see what the story is from their perspective.

Koreans have arrived in Base Camp and they're taking a flying jump for themselves; at least that's the name of their expedition – The Korean K2 Flying Jump Expedition. Seems to coin images of *Crouching Tiger, Hidden Dragon* bamboo-scaling techniques. Seem like a lovely bunch though, although a bit too busy for an impromptu cup of tea and a chat. Understandably eager to get settled in. To date in camp the litany of nationals sounds like the twelve days of Christmas – a team of four French, a 'team' of one Serbian, you'd have to meet him to understand why I say 'team', a team of twelve or so Koreans and ourselves, the only international one to date of one Nepalese, one Australian, five Dutch and one Irishman. Still have the Cesen route to ourselves – for now. We noticed the Serbian lad throwing a sheepish look towards it every now and again. And Sheena has made herself scarce – either the kitchen staff caught up to her nibbling ways or she's nursing the plague of mice that's soon to descend on us.

As Ger recognised, the South Korean team, the biggest on the mountain, had a more severe ethos than the other international expeditions. The fifteen-member team, lead by Kim Jae-soo, was very much climbing for the glory of South Korea, and took their international role very seriously. Three of the fifteen were three young sherpas from Nepal, brothers Jumik and Tsering

Bhote and their cousin Pasang Bhote. Ger would catch up with some old friends when the Norwegian K2 Expedition arrived, as among its four-person team were Rolf Bae and Cecilie Skog, with whom he had trekked across South Georgia the previous year on Pat Falvey's expedition. Rolf and Cecilie were leading Norwegian mountaineers, who ran an adventure travel company specialising in Arctic and Antarctic travel, and had been married for just over a year.

Besides the eight-person Norit K2 expedition, there was also an eight-person Serbian expedition on K2 (and an independent Serbian climber), and an eight-person American team – eight was a popular number as it allowed the team to climb in two groups of four. (Another American, Nick Rice, who was also a keen blogger, was climbing with the Frenchman Hugues.) The American team included anaesthetist Eric Meyer, whose special interest in high-altitude medicine would prove crucial to the survival of several climbers when disaster struck.

Ger's First Climb with Pemba – Everest, 2003

While waiting for the weather to clear on K2, Ger and Pemba had ample spare time to reminisce about the first time they climbed together, when Ger was part of the first Irish expedition to Everest. Pemba was the head sherpa, as recounted in Ger's 2003 journal:

> We landed in Kathmandu, all six of us – Clare O'Leary, George Shorten, Mick Murphy, Pat Falvey and Hannah Shields. All except for Pat and Mick were first-timers on Everest.
>
> From Kathmandu we boarded a smaller plane. It took us to Lukla and we walked the remainder of the way to Everest Base Camp. I'll never forget just how pleasant that walk in was, the scenery was beautiful. When I go walking in Alaska the mosquitoes attack you from time to time but here there was none of that. It felt like heaven. Of course the porters, of which there were many, with their yaks carried all our gear in, something that I could never get used to. So on our backs we had a light pack and were just rambling along the trail. It was the first time that I ever had anything like this done for me, these porters were my first ever experience of other people carrying my gear. I didn't like it but yet had to get over it.
>
> The whole trek to Base Camp took a good few days, I think four days into Base Camp after the plane ride. I will never forget my first few moments in Base Camp, I had a thumping headache

and I remember looking up to the summit and thinking if my head hurts this much at Base Camp what's it going to be like on the top? But I was assured that you do feel crap for a few days until your body acclimatises. It's easy to forget that Everest Base Camp is 17,500ft/5,300m in the air from the south side. You begin to look at a daunting ice field that you have to travel through but although it looks bad you can't help but look at the beauty of Everest; Lhotse and the surrounding views are fantastic.

You just had to relax, acclimatise and wait; thankfully there were lots of groups in Base Camp, which I loved. The different cultures and people that you get to meet, I had a great time going from tent to tent on my rest days and drinking tea and socialising. On the downside of all this, the mountain does sadly claim many lives each season.

At Base Camp more Irish visitors had arrived; the Crowley brothers, Darragh, Shane and Cian, from Dublin were on an adventure of their own. In aid of the cystic fibrosis charity Drive for Life the brothers and their support team were on a 35,400km/22,000 mile drive from Melbourne, Australia, to Ireland aiming to raise funds to help sufferers of the lung disease, to raise awareness of cystic fibrosis and of the need to carry a organ donor card to increase the number of life-saving lung transplants. They brought a hurley to Base Camp in an attempt to convince one of the Irish team to puck a sliotar from the mountain.

A long puck competition was held and Ger was deemed the winner. Although he was happy to bring the hurley to the summit if the weather allowed, it was decided that it was too dangerous at that time and so Ger decided to hit the sliotar from the 8,027m/26,334ft South Col.

On Everest 2003 there was a long wait for a weather window that would allow the Irish expedition to make a bid for the summit. The night before, those attempting the climb from the South Col had been forced to turn back in the face of unstable weather. The next night at 8 p.m. Pemba reported that it was a good night for a summit attempt, and those members of the team who were fit enough set off, as Ger describes in his log.

A vigil of headlights snaked peacefully up the couloir. The fact that roughly half the people who attempted the previous night had descended earlier that day made the fixed lines notably safer. Our head sherpa's guess was that about fifty people attempted from the

Ger (right) receives the hurley and sliotar from Shane Crowley from the Drive for Life team at Base Camp, Everest, in 2003.

south side that night and over a hundred the night before. But the climbing was still slow, exceedingly slow, and was to get even slower as we approached the Balcony and beyond. Many what seemed like slow climbers in front of us. Would this prove to be a problem? I would turn to ask Nima from time to time if we were ascending at summit speed. He responded initially with, 'I don't know. I've never been on the summit.' We both laughed at the answer …

The Balcony approached and the slow speed at which the line progressed began to play on my nerves. There seemed to be no explanation for the delays. My fingers began to get cold but not

Ger crossing a crevasse between camps in the Western Cwm.

Ger with the Drive for Life hurley and Hannah Shields with Freddie T. Bear.

dangerously so. I knew from previous experience that they could afford to get much colder before I needed to worry. They would come back easily from where they were. If need be, I could always put on the clumsy large pair of mitts, but it wasn't cold enough yet for that. Climbing faster would be the ticket but just then I noticed stars to the east begin to fade to a morning sky. The sun would be up soon enough. I was now standing on the Balcony. This is where we would change to our second bottle of oxygen. I was looking forward to our arranged regroup and seeing how everybody was doing ...

The sun hadn't quite risen yet but it was light enough to prompt a visual check of where each team member was. Pat, of course, was just directly in front of me as we climbed now, together with Pemba Rinjee and Nima. There were fifteen or so climbers between us and Hannah and Chombi, and Mick wasn't too far ahead of them. All were within our sights. But progress seemed to grind almost to a standstill. Some climbers were making heavy work of simple rock scrambling. But the views were a major consolation. They were magic. Mountains swept over the landscapes beneath us on either side of the ridge. Tibet to our right, Nepal to our left, and sharing the experience with friends I had came to know and love over the previous two months – what could be better? 'This is awesome, Pat,' I muffled through the mask, 'that we're here after all this time.' Pat turned. Signs of a smile stretched beyond his mask in agreement ...

There was an air of change in the weather. The rising sun seemed to entice the wind. Again I checked the proceedings in the line ahead. While doing so I noticed Hannah and Chombi were busy organising themselves. For what? What were they doing? Were they having problems with their oxygen? 'Hannah is hardly ... no,' I thought. Hannah was preparing to descend. My heart sank as I saw them approach. I knew what the problem was. She was suffering from the cold. But by how much? We were to learn later that she had frost-nipped fingertips and minor frostbite on some of her toes. She was making the right choice. Gallantly she delivered her reason for turning in a matter-of-fact manner as she hugged Pat and myself. 'I'm getting cold and I think if I continue I'll just get into trouble. It's not worth it,' she professed. I feared at the time that she might be hiding the severity of symptoms so we wouldn't worry about her descent with Chombi. Or even worse (in her mind), that one of us might decide to descend with her. She kept the conversation brief, decisive and to the point. They were gone. [On 18 May 2007 Hannah became the first Northern Irish woman to reach the summit of Mount Everest.] …

Slowly we were to pass the rockier section of the south summit – the first Bottleneck. Climbers began to spread out now in front of Pat. These climbers were no longer the reason for our slow pace; Pat himself was beginning to have some difficulty. 'Pat, we are going to have to pick up the pace.' 'Right,' he says, but if anything he was gradually getting slower. So I suggested that we temporarily turn up his oxygen flow until we reached the south summit. This is a common practice but more usually done on, we'll say, the Hillary Step. With this there was no significant increase in his speed. 'Slow but OK,' Nima would say. Finally we reached the south summit. And no sooner had we done so when Nima tapped me on the shoulder and gently said, 'OK, fast now.' 'Pat, I'm going for it,' I said as I unclipped, and for the first time I began to pass people on the fixed line. Nima stayed behind with Pat. At that point Pat seemed to me only to be displaying signs of tiredness. Pemba Rinjee continued ahead and encouraged me to pass out climbers on the line. He beckoned with a smile of great enthusiasm. We were now travelling faster than anyone else. But was Pat going to be able to pick the pace up to this level? I didn't think so. Ordinarily yes, I thought, but not today.

However, at that point I was still confident that Pat had the reserves to make it to the summit. Pemba encouraged me deeper into the line ahead, and he and I were now travelling ten times faster than we had in the line. We were making great progress until we reached the step – a major bottleneck. Descending climbers were now added to the mix. Slowly we snaked our way through. Still no sign of Mick. The slower climbers between Mick and ourselves while heading up the south summit must have created a significant distance between us.

I found myself breathing heavily now with the rapid pace we were setting. With just a few more paces I recognised the two climbers descending towards us – Pemba Gyalje and Mick. Jubilation and euphoria summed up the moment. I knew by their step that they had just come from the summit. I congratulated Mick and Pemba – and they were pretty much already congratulating us. 'You're just five minutes away,' Mick said jubilantly, 'it's right there.'

I looked up. There it indeed was – a delicate peak on such a noble mountain.

At this point you're walking – not much climbing – until you get to the Hillary Step. This was the next bottleneck; there were people coming down now who had already summited and there were others waiting to go up. People were trying to pass each other out. You just wait, but eventually I was tired of waiting and said to Rinjee, 'Look, I'm not waiting any longer, I'm heading up this way.' I went up a particular way but the sirdar or head sherpa wasn't too happy with my actions. However, I figured I had waited long enough for it to clear so basically I went up and around the climbers at the top of the Hillary Step. Pemba Gyalje, Pemba Rinjee and Mick were still there. Pemba Gyalje was part of the leading party setting up fixed ropes to the top, so he had a big day under his belt at that point. The conversation between the two sherpas alarmed me. They were very concerned over something and it was obvious that it was breaking into an argument. One sherpa pulled out a bottle of oxygen so they started to give me a new bottle but as they were doing that the bottle was leaking; the threads I guess had accumulated ice and so it hadn't created a perfect seal. A fairly substantial hiss was coming from the bottle. It was obvious we couldn't leave it like that so we unscrewed it again and tried to screw it back in properly. We went through this procedure several times. So we decided to swap our regulators so I had a system that was working perfectly and my sherpa had a system with a slight hiss but thankfully not any way as loud as previously. The sirdar who has the last word pointed at Rinjee and said, 'You go down.' To my mind he was on the summit but he didn't actually stand on it but it was right there. He went down, but I remember being a little more than concerned about this slight hissing noise.

Pemba Gyalje and I went to the summit, and when we arrived I certainly was elated. At 11.11 a.m. on 22 May Pemba and I stood on top of the world. We hugged, shook hands and cheered. The clouds and plume from the ridge would part momentarily to reveal the overwhelming sights from below, several thousand feet to either side – like a floating altar 29,000ft [9,000m] in the sky. I thought of my family, close friends and relations, my parents, my brother and sisters. I imagined them all standing next to me as my eyes panned the views around the summit. Awesome views unfolded through gaps in the cloud. I thanked the mountain for allowing me to stand on its summit. For no mountain is ever conquered. It is only through the mountain's will that we can ever hope to summit and there we were. I thanked God, I knew I would reflect back on this moment for the rest of my life and sure enough the mood and the sights are in my dreams regularly.

7. FURTHER DELAY ON K2 (AND BRINGING HURLING TO EVEREST)

The weather on K2 in the summer of 2008 continued to deteriorate, but after two days, on 18 June, the rope situation had improved, as Ger recounts in his journal.

Well, we were obviously spoiled with good weather up to now. And the time for the unsettled stuff has descended upon us. Feels more like precipitous Loop Head in west Clare than anywhere at altitude. Not very cold at all here, but damp – ambient 7 °C [45 °F] or so and humidity, according to the nifty Kestrel 4000 [a pocket weather tracker], 64.1 per cent. That's very damp for this altitude methinks. The forecast announced that the mood is to last to the weekend. The jet stream apparently is affecting altitudes as low as 6,500m/21,000ft. So we're all waiting patiently. And the number of those waiting patiently here in Base Camp has grown substantially from what it was four days ago. Another Serbian team arrived today. As did a Russian team and a motley crew of individuals that have joined together on an impromptu permit. Good news on the rope situation – two teams have responded to posts on the Norit site, an Italian team and an American team. The Italians, Abruzzi Route, haven't arrived yet but tell us that they'll provide us with the rope for the Bottleneck. The Americans, who are planning to do Broad Peak first and then the Cesen, have a substantial amount of fixed line, all of which they say we're free to use. Plus there's the rope that is speeding its way here on the back of a nimble porter. So we'll have plenty to choose from by the time the weather clears.

Inshallah as they say here. More it seems than we'll need. In the meantime we're fighting off the boredom by playing chess, reading, sewing, and repairing stuff, chatting with the new neighbours and such like. For the most part, then, we retire in the early evening to the solitary confines of our tents for some lonely ownsome time. That is, until the kitchen lads bang a metal plate with a spoon and we all come running like hungry calves in midwinter. Running to their latest incarnation of dahl and such like. To the kitchen staff's credit though they've been doing an outstanding job at keeping things diverse and tasty. Food can be crucial of course to the team morale and the pizza surprise that was produced at lunchtime faded any concerns we might have had about the bad weather. There's fear of us.

On 24 June Pemba sent a greeting to his family and friends from K2. At last the weather seemed to be giving some respite.

> Namaste! I am praying with god that all my family members and friends are well. All climbers are fine from our team. The weather is improving on the mountain after many days, allowing one climbing team to depart to Camp 2 early morning today, they are trying to set up Camp 3. A second team will depart Camp 2 on 25 June, then our team will try to trail break, climbing en route between Camp 3 and Camp 4. We hope the weather and our health will be in good favour to us, see you again.

Everest Expedition 2003

When Pemba Gyalje stood on the summit of Everest on 22 May 2003 it was his sixth conquest of Everest. Ger's own sherpa was also named Pemba – Pemba Rinjee. On the summit of Everest Ger held close a set of rosary beads his mother had given him in Dublin Airport; they were his father's. After reaching the summit, Ger had only a few moments to take it all in. His mind was otherwise occupied. Firstly there was the matter of Pat's welfare that was concerning him greatly: 'Pat was in trouble. That was evident from the first moment I saw him on the descent. From 30 feet away, I could see that we had rescue on our hands. Pat had cerebral oedema.'

Then there was the matter of the leaking oxygen cylinder that Ger had been forced to swap over reluctantly with his sherpa. The head sherpa, Pemba Gyalje, had insisted that Ger take the one that was working properly. As he made his way off the summit he could see that his own sherpa, Pemba Rinjee, was in serious trouble as the pronounced hissing sound became louder and louder, the result of oxygen escaping from the sherpa's tank supply. Sitting down on the hardened ice, Ger eventually managed to resolve the problem and get both tanks fully operational.

At this point Pat was already being assisted by Pemba Gyalje. En route down to high camp they had to endure a white-out and each perilous step had to be painstakingly negotiated with extreme and patient care. When they finally came into camp, Ger took care of Pat's medicine and made sure he had enough nourishment to continue down the mountain safely. They could not afford to spend any more time than necessary in the 'death zone', above 8,000m/26,000ft where the body is effectively dying. By the time they reached Advance Base Camp (ABC), Pat's spirits and health had improved dramatically and to his credit he was the first to rejoice in the summit success that had been achieved by Ger and Mick.

This was the expedition that formed the close bond between Ger and Pemba Gyalje. Ger recalled this part of the descent in an interview with West Limerick 102 local radio.

> So I spent only, I guess, a minute or two there, it didn't feel long at all – time passes by very strangely up there! What may seem like a few seconds could truly have been minutes. I took a moment to think of my family. I held the rosary beads belonging to my father and I thought about him. I thought about my achievement and thought about what others had done to get me here. Once I summited I kept thinking about Rinjee's oxygen bottle; the argument of the sherpas previously was a distraction to me – the hissing from the bottle was at the forefront of my mind. I was fairly concerned about it and I wanted to descend quickly to him and when we caught up with him he was climbing very slowly and running out of oxygen. I took off my mask and said 'we'll share it', but he point blankly refused. You'd swear I'd insulted his mother! The other thing that struck me, too, was the number of people that looked like they were in trouble. They seemed to be going very slowly and I was taken aback by the number that looked like they needed to be rescued. I said, 'My God, how do we help them all?' I looked down along the line and could see who I thought was Mick Murphy. He was wearing the same colour suit as Pat but as we were getting closer I could see it was Pat and he was in trouble. We caught up with Pat at the base of the

south summit on the Hillary Step side of it and Pemba Gyalje and I short-roped Pat – that's basically literally a short rope, the idea of which is that if a person falls you'd be able to catch them – down the south summit. Then I took over because, as I said previously, Pemba Gyalje was after a big day up to that point and I knew he had to be getting tired so I just took over for a while; I short-roped Pat myself almost the whole way down to the end of the fixed lines.

Pat was stopping from exhaustion every so often; he'd fall from time to time, but at the time it was obvious to me that he was strong enough to make it down the mountain. I was worried about him all right but I wasn't worried that he wouldn't make Camp 4; I knew he'd make that. All the time the two sherpas waited behind to help others and when they caught up with us I told them, 'Look, we don't have far to go. I'm going to run down to high camp and make sure that medicine is available for him.' I climbed down to the end of the fixed line, and as sure as I did a thick cloud started to crawl across and visibility was down to three, maybe four, metres. You couldn't see more than that. All you could do was sit down and wait, and hope that it would clear. The one mistake I made was I didn't have my compass with me and I waited and waited and waited. I was probably waiting half an hour; that'll tell you just how slow things were progressing above me. When the others met me they just sat down beside me and said nothing. Eventually we made it down and Pat was being administered meds at that point. He started to perk up and it began to dawn on him just how successful this trip had become: he'd got two Irishmen standing on the summit of Everest. It was his expedition and there was no doubt that without his leadership we wouldn't have made it. He was showing signs of cerebral oedema; one of his problems was his sight going and he was becoming hypoxic.

Thankfully by the time we reached Advance Base Camp he was in great spirits; the group were singing and rejoicing. There was a good friend of mine at ABC, Vernon Theos – he's an Alaskan mountain guide with an American team – he said he'd never seen such a party at lower camp after a summit. He couldn't believe we were capable of partying, singing or cheering! It was only at this point that it really kicked in for me that we had done it. We still had to get through the ice fields; it wasn't over until it was over. We had to negotiate our way down through that but thankfully that went well. Everyone was at Base Camp; there were hugs and tears, singing and celebrating that night.

For me personally to have scaled Everest it was a privilege. I've been there, and to see what it's like from the top is really very personal. I don't go around telling people that I've done it; I am always shy in that respect. I don't think about it too often but when I do I might imagine myself back on the summit, what it was like and how I felt the few moments I was there. I was really just delighted that everything went right for me on the day and it does take a lot of stuff to go right for you. If things start to go wrong what was an easy climb for someone becomes extraordinary or impossible. There's a little booklet on Everest that I love, it's a five- or ten-minute read but the guy that wrote it is a bit of a philosopher, with a very down-to-earth approach as to what climbing Everest is about. He's got interesting titles to each chapter – one is 'Remember there are better climbers than you that haven't made it' while another chapter is titled 'Remember there are worse climbers than you that have made it'. There's an Indian climber who says that Everest can let the feeblest of women on its summit and yet can wipe the strongest men from its shoulder! You're not necessarily an extraordinary climber if you summit but you're a very fortunate one.

Clare O'Leary remembers the details of the Everest expedition.

The Irish Everest 2003 was a major expedition; it comprised a team of climbers and friends attempting to become the first Irish team to summit Everest from the south side. Everything in the planning, logistics and lead-up was new and exciting. The support from friends and enthusiasts was amazing and the walk in and out of Base Camp was made all the more enjoyable by the company of Irish trekkers.

I turned back somewhere between Camp 2 and 3 on the summit bid. I had been sick for two days prior, and in retrospect maybe everyone other than myself realised that I wouldn't be making the summit. I had returned to Base Camp when the rest of the team went for the summit. It was a tense time with poor communication. The team had made an initial summit bid but turned because of high winds. This would have depleted oxygen reserves somewhat. When they decided to make a second summit bid the following night it was hard not to feel anxious. We had very limited contact with the team because of difficulties in charging radio batteries and poor coverage.

For hours all we knew was that Ger and Mick had summited, Hannah had turned because of frostbite and Pat was not accounted for. His last radio call to Base Camp was to say that he was exhausted and that he was going to sit and wait at the south summit until the team was returning. It sounded like a death sentence. We didn't speak to them again for several hours and when Ger spoke to me about Pat it was obvious he was very concerned – and possibly the only one who realised the gravity of the situation. Pat had developed high-altitude cerebral oedema because of a fault with the delivery system on his oxygen cylinder. It was Ger who, with the assistance of Pemba Gyalje and Pemba Rinjee, assisted Pat down to the safety of high camp. Things could have gone very wrong very quickly only for Ger's quick reactions.

The expedition finished a success with Ger and Mick's summits; we all had lots of fun, plenty of *craic* and were left with a very close bond to one another.

As Pat, Mick, Ger and the sherpas made the final trek into Base Camp they were welcomed by John Joyce, who had been manning the communications, along with Clare and Hannah. Great cheers were heard and Ger was handed a beer and, with the tricolour wrapped around his neck, he danced a jig for Ireland.

On the Tuesday, Ger and the other team members were airlifted from Base Camp to the comfort of Kathmandu. On its very next flight, that helicopter crashed, killing three people. One of the Irish newspapers headlined: 'Everest Victor Cheats Death'.

At the hotel in Kathmandu, Ger and the Irish team and every one of the support team shook hands and hugged each other. Ger caught the eye of a man sitting in a corner of the room, but it wasn't until he gave a second glance that he realised with great joy that it was his brother J. J., who had made the trip from Ireland to congratulate him. J. J. recalls the story.

Liadain Slattery, a close friend of Ger's, made the necessary arrangements for me to travel to Kathmandu. She had planned to accompany me but Pat Falvey said he'd rather she stayed in Ireland as there was lots of work to be done to get the team and the equipment home. So I departed on my own on Sunday 24 May and couldn't wait to be with Ger to share the joy of the occasion with him. When I reached Kathmandu I got a taxi to the hotel which Liadain had booked for me – the same hotel in which the Irish Everest team and the support trekking group were staying. When I went into reception I heard an Irish voice in the foyer, which I must say I was shocked to hear as I had not expected any of the team or support trekkers to be there at that time. It had been my intention to stay overnight in the hotel, get a flight to Lukla and then a helicopter up to Base Camp. I did not realise until much later how cockeyed an idea this was but I just wanted to surprise Ger so much. I introduced myself to a lady in the lobby, who told me she was Grainne Willis, a reporter on the trek. She informed me that Pat, Clare and Mike Murphy were in the hotel but that Ger and Hannah were not coming until the following morning. She went to the back room to tell the group that I was in reception.

Pat Falvey arrived out to reception and threw his arms around me in a profoundly sincere embrace. The tears formed in his eyes as he recounted how Ger had saved his life. 'I am so proud of him,' he said. He repeated these words and I knew immediately that this was raw emotion spilling out. He gripped me for some time and said how proud he was to have met Ger and to have him on his team and how much of a team player he was. I was deeply moved by Pat's words and could feel the sincerity and passion in his voice as he spoke about Ger. I then met Clare and empathised with her about her unfortunate gastroenteritis which prevented her from making the summit. I went on to meet the remainder of the group, each one telling me what a great guy Ger was and how proud I must be for him.

Pat then explained that they had been airlifted from Base Camp by helicopter but that due to shortage of space Ger and Hannah would be travelling here in the morning. I explained to Pat that I had intended to go to Base Camp and had not expected them to be out, but he told me that the cost of that would have been prohibitive and in any case I might have missed them.

The following morning was filled with drama as news broke of the helicopter crash at Base Camp; the pilot, co-pilot and a climber were killed. Pat decided not to inform me of this as he wanted to get confirmation first as to Ger and Hannah's position. Having learned that they were airlifted out on the previous flight, he related the news. I thanked God that Ger and Hannah were safe and that I had listened to Pat about the helicopter trip to Base Camp.

Suddenly a call came to reception that Hannah and Ger were in a taxi on their way to the hotel, and the team and trekkers gathered together in reception to greet them. I decided to sit back in a corner just in sight of the door. The door opened and in walked Hannah and Ger. Ger was beaming and as he embraced everyone in turn he glanced a number of times in my direction. Then suddenly it registered that it was me. It still brings a tear to my eye when I think about his reaction: 'Jeeeeez, J.' I could feel the strength still in his arms as he embraced me. He couldn't believe I was there and asked how I had got out so quickly, had I planned it all the time. I explained that I simply could not resist going out to see him when I got the news. He was in incredible form and glad to be back in the comfort of the hotel.

Ger was so looking forward to a hot shower, a square meal and a few sociable drinks. When I told him I was staying in the same hotel he insisted I share his room as it was a twin. I sat down on the bed, explaining how in Limerick he was seen as a hero and that there was euphoria about him hitting the sliotar. He couldn't believe it and kept asking if I was telling the truth. Before the victory dinner, Ger headed off for a haircut and beard trim as he looked like a wild man. At dinner the form was magnificent, and you could see that the iron man, Falvey, was gaining strength from hour to hour. After the meal we went for a few drinks and Ger got his just rewards.

Over the next twenty-four hours I spoke to Ger about the trip and what was characteristically noticeable was his concern for all the others on the team; he spoke very little about himself.

I asked Ger about Pat and explained how he had embraced me with tears in his eyes. Ger was very hesitant to speak about it and was visibly upset recounting the story. He had thought that Pat would not make it and, as for his heroism in saving him, it was simply not in Ger's nature to pass anyone in trouble.

A few days later and the sliotar story had captured the imagination of the Irish press, who reported that an Irishman had pucked a sliotar from the summit of the world. Ger was furious and immediately had the story rectified.

I was given a hurley by a group called Drive for Life and they were raising funds for cystic fibrosis. Their plan was to hold the world's highest *poc fada* and where else but Everest. When Drive for Life asked if I'd be interested in doing it, I was all over it. The idea of having a hurley in Base Camp was great, so they gave me the stick to take to the summit. After that it was to be auctioned off for charity. I took the hurley up most of the way. En route the sherpas were asking me about the stick hanging out of my bag, and when I explained what it was they thought I was crazy. I brought it up to the South Col and decided that with the weather being so bad I wasn't going to risk a successful summit attempt because of a hurley. The little things up there are heavy due to the altitude. So I left it at the South Col but before we descended I took out the sliotar and pucked it into China somewhere, just for a laugh.

Shane Crowley of Drive for Life remembers how they convinced Ger to carry the hurley and sliotar and how it helped their campaign raise some €400,000 for charity.

My brother Cian and I first met Ger at the Ama Dablam Lodge en route to Everest Base Camp. We had heard that the Irish Everest Expedition team 2003 were about and decided to seek them out for a bit of *craic*.

We got chatting to Ger and explained that we were ourselves in the middle of the Drive for Life project raising funds for cystic fibrosis, by driving overland from Melbourne to Dublin. Our route had taken us to Kathmandu where we met up with family and good friends who were joining us on our fund-raising trek to Base Camp. And we had in our possession a hurl which we were taking to Base Camp to use in a *poc fada* competition we had planned.

Ger told us how he was preparing to summit in the coming weeks as soon as the weather allowed and how he was planning to bring a bodhrán with him to the summit. We jokingly suggested that he bring the hurl to the top instead. But as soon as this was uttered we could see a glint in his eye as he joked about how he could make it to the top with the hurl, have a swing at the sliotar, miss it completely, and watch it trickle all the way back down. As we were leaving the lodge he told us that he was actually serious about taking the hurl to the summit and that if we were happy for him to attempt this he would return it to us afterwards. He suggested we auction it off to help with our fund-raising efforts.

We all departed with buoyed sprits from the encounter, and agreed to meet up a few days later where we were to have the first ever *poc fada* competition at Base Camp. This, needless to say, Ger ended up winning in style! We left Base Camp that evening, having handed over the hurl to Ger and arranged to meet up again back in Kathmandu where we would hopefully be toasting to Ger's summit success and to the first hurl to make it up Everest.

On 22 May 2003, Gerard McDonnell became the fourth and youngest Irishman to reach the summit of Mount Everest. This tremendous achievement was made even more remarkable by the fact that he carried with him the hurl as he ascended the great mountain.

Ger carried the hurl as far as the South Col, which is situated close to the summit at approximately 8,000m/26,000ft. From there he made history as he launched a sliotar across a void and into Tibet!

Subsequently we met up with Ger and the Everest hurl returned safely home to Ireland on a wave of publicity. A documentary was aired on RTÉ 1 television in August 2004 that told the story of Drive for Life and the 'Everest hurl'.

In the months that followed, the then President of Ireland, Mary McAleese, and Sir Edmund Hillary, the first man to conquer Everest in 1953, would recognise Ger's achievement by signing the hurl. It also carries the signatures of Ger and the rest of the Irish Everest Expedition team 2003, including that of Clare O'Leary, who in 2004 became the first Irish woman to summit Mount Everest. This unique piece of memorabilia was eventually auctioned to raise money for the charity.

In the days that followed, the Irish newspapers had stories about the team's success, with pictures in due course. Ireland was proud of its newest adventurers.

Some time later, Ger was asked again about Pat's illness on the mountain. 'By the time I had reached him he was sitting down. I offered him some water and when I saw the look on Pat's face, there was no energy there and also knowledge that he knew himself he was in trouble. I got all that from one look; he kept saying how proud he was of Mick and me, the fact we had summited and it was a success.'

Pat Falvey was certainly glad he had brought Ger on his expedition to Everest.

Taking Ger as a team member on this expedition is a decision I will always be grateful for, as Ger, Pemba Gyalje and Pemba Rinjee helped save my life on that very expedition. They gave their energy and time to help convince me to abandon my summit attempt, while I was in a critically hypoxic state. I developed these conditions due to a faulty oxygen connection on the final leg of the summit attempt. I had to turn just 100ft [30m] from the top of the world. Descending that narrow ridge back to high camp I stumbled, tumbled and crawled down, at times on all fours, and all the while Ger and the two Pembas never left my side. I owe them a special debt of both gratitude and thanks, which I owe as well to the great work of all the rest of my teammates on that eventful day of my near journey to the top of the world.

After a few days of recovery and celebrations at Base Camp, as many on the team did make the summit that year, an enthusiastic Ger posed the question, 'What's next, Pat?' Already Clare O'Leary had asked if I would return for a fourth time to Everest in 2004. In these conversations with Ger and Clare a longer-term plan was hatched to finalise Clare's Seven Summits Challenge, with the exciting idea of going to the South Pole in honour of our Irish polar explorers. Ger's eyes lit up at the mere mention of Antarctica. 'Count me in if you're going,' he said.

8. WEATHER DESPAIR ON K2 (AND EVEREST HOMECOMING AND INTERVENING TRIPS)

By 24 June 2008 Base Camp on K2 consisted of several hundred tents as the camp swelled with new international team arrivals and some additions to older residents.

It had been a frustrating time on the mountain with the steady decline in weather delaying the main summit attempt. Time was spent improving the camp site, socialising, and included a visit to the Gilkey Memorial, a memorial cairn erected to Art Gilkey, the American mountaineer who died on K2 in 1953. The Gilkey Memorial has since become the burial place of other climbers who have died on K2, as well as a memorial to those whose bodies have not been found. When the weather improved, further progress could be made.

Back to the original plan before the weather put a stop to our gallop. Wilco, Cas, Jelle and Roeland are up at Camp 2 and hope to complete the approx 200m/650ft of lines to Camp 3 tomorrow. It'll be very much an investigative jaunt too as binoculars from Base Camp obviously can't tell much of the snowpack story. Granted, we've waited a seemingly ample amount of time for the snow to settle and watched a lot of the recent accumulation slough off, in major amounts at times, but you can never be too sure. So Pemba, Court, Sheeny and myself head to Camp 2 tomorrow and, all going well, Camp 3 the following day. Wilco, Cas, Jelle and Roeland will come down to Base Camp while we try to spend a couple of days fixing to Camp 4.

The sobering Gilkey Memorial, about a mile from K2 Base Camp, which commemorates those who have died on the mountain.

Unfortunately the weather was to turn against Ger and his team again and six days later, despite some early progress, they were once again put back by the elements. The slowdown in progress also had a negative effect on Ger's acclimatisation.

> Well, through our last escapade to K2's heights we managed to establish Camp 3, at approx. 7,100m/23,300ft, and 300m/1,000ft of fixed lines or so above. The loss of acclimatisation from twiddling thumbs in Base Camp through the bad weather spell was obvious for some – most notably the group formerly known as 'Team 2'. Personally I found myself decorating the snow intermittently from Camp 2 to 3 with ungodly amounts of rejected breakfast, more than I remembered consuming. Lovely. But once at Camp 3 the sensation of having been vomiting all day dissipated and a couple of us took to building a second tent platform. Pemba and Cas did the excellent job of fixing 300m/1,000ft of line above camp. And only

after sweating for three hours over the platform did we discover that the second tent was minus the poles. Great. This led to a somewhat uncomfortable night's rest for four in one tent on a bad platform where we wished more than anything else that Sheeny hadn't eaten that raw sausage. The plan the following morning was for me and Pemba to continue fixing. But the weather put the kybosh on that idea and so we peeled out of the cramped enclosure and descended to Camp 2. The poles fortunately were found 50m/165ft or so below Camp 3 – 20m/65ft or so from the fixed line. Lucky! Some of us decided to stay at Camp 2 for a night to reboost lost acclimatisation rather than descending all the way to Base Camp. All of us were down in Base Camp the following day though and we learned of a coming weather window that was about to yawn over the summit for a few days. To make the most of it, a pre-summit party would go up in the not-so-great weather, the day before the summit party and minimise the summit party's efforts by doing such things as breaking trail, carrying the newly acquired heavy rope to Camp 1, which would be used to replace the lighter 5mm Spectra [cord] that the summit party would use to fix above 3, setting up the second tent at Camp 3 and possibly doing some additional rope fixing above Camp 3. The pre-summit party consisted of Roeland, Court and Sheeny. The plan/weather gave us a few days' rest in Base Camp before the lads set off.

Six days later, after the first summit attempt had not progressed as planned, Ger and his teammates were kicking their heels in Base Camp once again. However, they were thankful when another near disaster on the mountain ended well.

The first summit push didn't go quite according to plan. But to be honest we're not too disappointed with the status – fixed lines to 200m/650ft or so below the shoulder. We've cached 400m/1,300ft of 5mm Spectra bottleneck rope at top anchor along with Camp 4 provisions, two tents, gas etc. From the start of the summit push it was evident that things weren't going to go according to plan. The tracks of the previous day's support party were gone with the wind, and the trail had to be broken again. Not a major problem. The biggest shock though was while ascending through the traverse below Camp 2 when we met a descending Court who briefed us on a very near miss. Roeland had survived carbon monoxide poisoning that morning and was still recovering from the ordeal. He'd passed out while cooking in the tent at Camp 2 and remained unresponsive for over five minutes or so. Luckily Court had been sharing the tent with Roeland. Roeland started cooking with an MSR Reactor [stove] hanging inside a somewhat ventilated tent. Court first noticed Roeland with greatly impaired coordination when he was trying to pour water from the first boil into a bottle and was instead spilling it directly on the tent floor. Just as soon as Court took over the job Roeland passed out. Immediately suspecting carbon monoxide, Court opened both vestibules, turned off the stove and shouted to Sheeny in the neighbouring tent for help. All they could do was hope Roeland would respond to the fresh air. And thankfully after five minutes or so he came around, albeit weak and groggy for a couple of hours afterwards. Court had been lying lower and closer to the ventilation and talking to Roeland as he was melting water. Roeland had been sitting up close to the hanging stove. One of the vestibules was open but there obviously wasn't a sufficient cross-flow. The MSR Reactor is an extremely efficient stove and commands much respect when cooking inside a tent. Lesson learned. Roeland is alive, thank God.

That experience aside, Court was continuing to have problems with his legs and had decided to return to Base Camp. Roeland obviously was out of commission after his inadvertent huffing experience and was descending to regain his strength. Sheeny couldn't do much by himself so it made sense for him to descend also or, much more to the point, it was best for someone to keep an eye on Roeland. This left the summit party with more work to do – not that it bothered us in the least; we were all more than shocked at Roeland's experience to remotely care about any additional work that lay ahead.

Slept in Camp 2 that night with the deep gratitude and relief that Roeland was still with us. The following day trail breaking to Camp 3, set up the second tent and shared out fixing equipment for Camp 4 and Bottleneck jaunt. Morning at Camp 3 broke with a stiff wind. So we waited a couple of extra hours before setting off, in the hope that the wind would lapse a little with the rising sun. It did, but there was still a stiff enough wind for the first few hours of fixing ropes that challenged anything dexterous. Progress through the day was slow. Pockets of deep snow (chest deep at times), packs laden with fixed-line equipment, Camp 4 provisions and increasing altitude were all taking their toll. Eventually the grim reaper of 'progress for the day' raised its ugly head once more – we ran out of fixed line again. There was nothing for it only to abort the summit bid, cache everything at the top anchor and return to Camp 3. We'd agreed that there was no way we'd touch the line allocated for the Bottleneck and Traverse. Misinformation is a frustrating thing. We received many a good piece of advice on the route. But when it came to recommended amounts of fixed line we were more than once advised to take much less than required. So it is on routes not so frequently climbed. Part of the adventure. More cause for celebration when things go right.

That evening we returned to Camp 3 by headlight. Onlookers in Base Camp signalled with their head torches. We signalled back. Later we learned that it was Sheeny just trying to communicate with his teammates. 'G'day guys, we see you.' It didn't exactly come across in the Morse code, as opposed to our 'blah blah blah' which came across more clearly. So we've been hanging out here in Base Camp now since midday, 6 July. Back socialising and surfing through the various camps passing the while away and hoping for another weather window soon. There have been rumours that the weather is thinking about dealing us a break around the 18th, full moon.

Ger also had time to catch up with the welfare of the mouse he had named Sheena, whose presence had caused such amusement earlier in the expedition:

In camp – Sheena lives. Looks like she's lost an amount of weight, somewhat equivalent to a half dozen micelets and I suppose in the not-too-distant future we can expect some of her offspring to be frequenting the dining area. Some of us have taken to serenading her with the Ramones' 'Sheena is a punk rocker'. Although she seems indifferent to our entertaining efforts.

Postal deliveries from home were reaching Base Camp and chocolates from friends along with sweets and holy water from his mother gave Ger a lift as they waited out the weather on K2, which had seen further setbacks on the climb.

Ger ascending the lower slopes of K2. (Courtesy Wilco van Rooijen)

Ger ascending the slopes of K2 outside Camp 2. (Courtesy Wilco van Rooijen)

Morale hit a new low for the team a few days ago when what appeared to be a possible weather window on the 18th vanished with the changing influences of the jet stream. High winds. No go. So we're still waiting on the weather. To kill some time four of us went on walkabout for a couple of days. Sheeny and I headed off to check out the Base Camp at Broad Peak across the glacier. Did us good to get out of Base Camp for a little while. On our return it was back to business and meetings with other teams that are ready for a summit attempt. Another meeting now in a couple of minutes so I'll keep this brief. Cooperation is looking good: the Koreans, Serbians, Italians and ourselves all seem to be on the same page. So better go. The lads are calling me. Meeting in the Serbian tent next door.

Fifty-six days after they had arrived in Base Camp, 23 July 2008, things were at last looking up for Ger and his fellow climbers with real expectation growing in the camp. After another week spent kicking their heels, a summit attempt seemed to be on the cards.

Our flags are showing signs of having braved the frequent high winds and damp conditions of this season. Some of our Tibetan prayer flags are all prayered-out, perhaps a good sign. Shoes that boasted a rugged prowess have scarcely enough rubber left on 'em for the walk out of here. Gaping holes abound – not only in some of our shoes but in clothes torn perhaps from the never-ending job of carting rocks to tent platforms to protect the ice foundations, good exercise anyway to avert muscle atrophy during the bad weather. Tent platforms now stand several metres higher relative to the walking path through camp. Both were practically level on our arrival fifty-six days ago, just counted. The bottoms of several barrels have begun to show. Barrels which had been full of consumables that we never imagined we'd come close to finishing. We've had a spate of bad weather forecasts and we were beginning to wonder if we'd get a chance at all this season. But a seemingly great window of opportunity is presenting itself. A seemingly long summit window that might start around the end of the month. And not a moment too soon. Our tentative departure date from Base Camp was on 2 August. We're more than happy to shift it a few days later for this chance to finally go for it after our failed first attempt circa 5 July. Morale in camp is very high. Electric. In stark contrast to a week ago. Four different weather reports proclaim the same window. There's a meeting scheduled on the 25th among teams ready for a summit bid. The plan is to compare weather reports and make a final decision on the date for a joint effort. It's looking either like the 31st or 1st will be the most suitable. At least from our forecast. Fingers crossed.

Homecoming From Everest

To all those watching and waiting for news on K2, Ger's homecoming on 4 June 2003 from his successful attempt to reach the summit of Everest was still fresh in their minds. Ger had become the fourth Irish person, and the youngest, to reach the summit of the world's tallest mountain as part of an all-Irish expedition.

Shortly after arriving in Cork Airport to a huge crowd, the Irish team embraced their families and friends. Ger scanned the crowds to see his mother and the entire family. What a sight it was, especially for Ger who had made history in more ways than one.

Ger embraces his mother, Gertie, on his return to Kilcornan after the Everest trip in 2003.

Pat Falvey and the team met the press and did their interviews and had photos taken, and then it was off to City Hall for a reception with the Lord Mayor of Cork. At this point Ger and the team were exhausted, but they knew they had a duty to fulfil with their audience. Speeches and thank-yous all followed. As Ger held his niece and goddaughter Rebecca in his arms, his mother, Gertie, whispered to him that they should be heading back home as a small group of children was expecting him in the primary school. And even though he was exhausted, Ger did not let the children down. They had followed his entire adventure on the Internet, so he agreed.

As Ger and the family headed back to Kilcornan, little did they know what was in store but as the entourage entered the village of Adare, Ger must have realised something was going on. A group of children with their parents were on the little roundabout in the centre of Adare village, waving the colours Ger knew only too well – the red and white of Kilcornan. At the head of the entourage was a jeep with a camcorder recording the entire 10km/8 mile trip down from Adare. Ger laughed heartily, taking it all in.

Arriving in Kilcornan, Ger and the family were overcome with emotion. Outside the entrance to Curraghchase Forest Park they were met by a group of parishioners, a bagpiper and a Garda escort. Ger was handed a Kilcornan flag and an Irish flag, and marched proudly behind the Garda car. The homecoming parade had begun.

Car horns were blown, music played loudly and locals cheered, and as Ger turned off the main N69 to enter the car park he saw the huge placard that read, 'Welcome Home Ger from the Top of the World'. There were tears in his eyes: he had never expected anything like this – the press, photographers, bonfires blazing and huge applause from the hundreds who turned out to welcome him home.

Ger was greeted at the entrance of the community hall by one of the main organisers of the event, Bridget Griffin, a former teacher of Ger's and a family friend. Locals, politicians and Cathaoirleach (Chairperson) Bridget Teefy all queued to enter the hall to congratulate Ger and hear him tell his story. During her opening speech Bridget Griffin described it as a very special occasion and a great honour for her to welcome Ger home to Kilcornan. Sitting down facing the filled hall, Ger's heart was pounding with both excitement and pride – Bridget said he had reached his innermost strengths and beliefs and had heroically conquered this mountain known as Everest.

She then asked Ger to say a few words. 'In my wildest dreams I could never have imagined a warmer welcome, so thank you so much,' he began. 'One thing I've always said over and over again is that I was privileged to be a part of this team. I've always climbed with different nationalities but I've never had the experience of climbing a big mountain with an Irish climber, let alone an entire team. I was really excited by that and the prospect of climbing with one of the first Irish females to summit Everest. I think both Hannah and Clare were unlucky: Clare suffered a stomach problem which ended her climb, Hannah had some circulation problems – had she a different layering system I've no doubt she could have summited. Both are strong ladies and I know both will summit Everest within the next few years. Pat Falvey was a wonderful leader and I've learnt a lot from his huge qualities. He listens to

Cathaoirleach of Limerick County Council, Brigid Teefy, presents Ger with an award in 2003 for being the first Limerick man to reach the summit of Everest.

all members and takes on board what they have to say; that's a sign of a true leader. I guess the low points on the trip were losing team members to illness.'

Somebody in the audience put up their hand and asked what was it like on the summit, to which Ger replied, 'It was a bit draughty! Seriously, it was very cold and the winds ranged from 15 to 25 miles per hour [25–40 km/h], and visibility wasn't great, unfortunately there was cloud on top. One of the main things about Everest was its summit; it's a bit like standing on a snooker table at 29,000 feet [9,000m]. The most important thing about any climb is getting back down; the longer you stay there, the more exposed to the elements you are. I thought about my family and my father and just paused for a second to think just how beautiful it was.' Then Ger shook his head as he looked around and repeated, 'This is truly amazing, I'm completely blown away. Thank you.'

Cathaoirleach Teefy then stood up to address Ger. 'It gives me great pleasure to congratulate Ger on his achievement. When I heard the announcement that Ger was successful, we were all thrilled. Ger is a hero who pushes the boundaries to achieve the impossible; we are lucky to have such a man walk in our midst, a man who climbed Everest on 22 May 2003, a week short of Sir Edmund Hillary's fiftieth anniversary. Ger has many humanitarian traits like Hillary: not many people know, but Ger in 1999 raised £15,000 for Milford Hospice while summiting Mount McKinley [Denali] in Alaska. Gerard is a role model for the youth today, he shows you if you have focus and a goal you can achieve what you want to. Gerard is also the first Limerick man to summit Everest, and with that Limerick County Council will be bestowing civic honours on Ger in recognition of this.' (Ger held this distinction until fellow Limerick man Mark Quinn reached the summit on 22 May 2011, aged twenty-six.)

TD Dan Neville addressed the crowd. 'What an excellent achievement. When someone has a feat to do, you say they have a mountain to climb. Well, Ger has climbed the biggest feat of them all. The parish of Kilcornan should be proud of the work you all did tonight to make this night a success. Well done.'

Kathleen Wixtead, the primary school principal, then took to the microphone. 'It's difficult to be a great man, but to be a great man among great men is harder. Gerard, you are up there with the best of explorers such as Crean and Shackleton, your name will be emblazoned in stone forever, you have been an inspiration to the children.' She then proceeded to hand Ger a framed picture of him in his climbing gear with some of the students.

The night continued with the heads of local organisations presenting Ger with different awards. It was a night that neither Ger nor his family could ever forget. Sitting at home later that night, Ger was in total disbelief at the display of support that he had received from his fellow parishioners. It made it all worthwhile.

In the next few weeks at home, Ger was a busy man: Limerick County Council invited him to the county chambers to have civic honours bestowed on him for his achievements. On the morning in question Ger decided that he would go for a quick walk and told his mother he would be back later. 'Don't forget we need to be in there for one o'clock,' she warned him. Ger smiled and agreed. As the morning passed there was still no sign of Ger; the family were all ready to go but the award recipient was nowhere to be seen. Suddenly, with minutes to spare, Ger arrived and apologised for his delay. His idea of a quick walk was a drive down to Killarney and a fast push up Corrán Tuathail – Ireland's highest mountain.

In the county chambers the buzz was evident. The hall was filled with various councillors and invited guests, along with Ger's mother Gertie and family members J. J., Martha, Stephanie and Denise.

Cathaoirleach Teefy welcomed them all and, smiling, she told her audience of the morning's trip to Corrán Tuathail. Ger thanked everyone involved for his award, and there then followed a question-and-answer session, which brought many laughs.

The Irish Everest team met with President Mary McAleese on their return to Ireland in 2003 (*l–r*): Pat Falvey, Freddie T. Bear, Clare O'Leary, President McAleese, Mick Murphy, George Shorten and Ger.

TD Dan Neville and local councillors David Naughton and Kevin Sheehan all made speeches. This ceremony was all the more emotional for the councillors as Ger's award was the last official function to be held at the council's O'Connell Street premises before the move to a new building in Dooradoyle.

The next day Ger and the McDonnell family headed for Dublin to join up with the Irish Everest Expedition team and meet with President McAleese in Áras an Uachtaráin. As the team and their families mingled on the front lawn of the President's home, the hurley, which was to be presented to Drive for Life that evening, was in plain sight. Ger lined up with the team and proudly shook hands with President McAleese; she listened to his story and said she was very impressed and that he was a 'modern-day Cú Chulainn'. Later in the week Ger was interviewed on RTÉ radio, again recounting the now-famous hurley story.

The following week, Ger, on the invitation of Coillte, was in Curraghchase to plant a Himalayan Birch for his achievement in conquering Everest. Ger posed for various pictures with his friends and family and dug the hole to plant the tree. It stands today in Curraghchase for all to see.

Shortly after, Ger was voted 'Limerick Person of the Month' for May, and on 1 June he headed off with some friends and family to Thurles to watch Limerick take on Waterford in the Munster hurling championship. During the half-time interval the announcer told the crowd that a celebrity was in attendance – the first Irishman to puck a sliotar from Mount Everest. It had been a remarkable year for Ger and his family.

The following November, having returned to Alaska for work, Ger was in a local restaurant having dinner organised by a friend , Kathryn Price. It was a loose-knit group of friends from the climbing community who got together once a month. At this party Ger was first introduced to Ann Starkey from upstate New York, now living in Alaska. This was Ger's first meeting with Annie, the woman who was to become his girlfriend for three years. An occupational therapist during the school year, and a keen long-distance runner who also took up climbing, she shared Ger's love of the outdoor life, In 2004, Ger's appetite for adventure surfaced again and this time it was a trip with a difference. China was the destination and an unclimbed, unnamed peak was the target. Ger was climbing leader on the team and he also helped to plan the ins and outs. Within a few shorts weeks of the trip, three people dropped out, which made for openings. Ger knew of Ann Starkey's interest in climbing and asked her if she was interested in this one. She accepted. By mid-July Ger was in the air heading for Kashgar via Beijing and Urumqi, arriving on 25 and 26 July respectively. After final preparations in Kashgar, their convoy of three Toyota Land Cruisers and one 6 x 6 rugged military vehicle headed southeast on the Silk Road towards Yecheng. The climb was to begin in early August and carry on for close to a month, with a finish date of 3 September.

The goal of the Kunlun 2004 expedition was to explore several unknown peaks of the Aksai Chin plateau with the aim of making first ascents of 6,000m/20,000ft peaks and scientific research in the form of geological data collection. After purchasing several political maps of Xinjiang Province, eventually the correct aviation charts for the area were found. These operational navigation charts (ONCs) are at a scale of 1:500,000, and tactical pilotage charts in the same series are at 1:250,000. Though one would never consider such a scale for something like Denali or Rainier (the highest mountain in Washington in the US), it is the best information publicly available for such an unexplored region. The charts are quite detailed but are meant for aircraft flying over the region rather than mountaineers on the ground. As they are based entirely on satellite data, they have disclaimers that peak heights may be off by as much as 300m/1,000ft.

The project was original because of the group's climbing style and the remoteness of the goal. With a drive overland of nearly 1,000km/620 miles from the nearest airport in Kashgar, once dropped off at Base Camp the climbers would be completely unsupported for nearly three weeks. Because of the altitude and isolation, there was no option to retreat, and though they would have communication, any rescue would be nearly a week away.

The cost of the expedition for the team was approximately $48,800, made up of international airfares ($15,000), local airfares ($5,000), ground transport

($6,950), liaison officer ($1,500), necessary permits (($3,500), accommodation ($800), local logistics ($2,510), local guides ($2,680), new equipment ($9,200) and foodstuffs ($1,660).

The following account of a typical day in China is from team member Randall Krantz.

> The high point of the ridge, heavily corniced from the high winds, was at 20,800ft [6,340m], but from that point it started to become clear that the broad peak at the head of the cwm [a bowl-shaped mountain basin caused by glaciation] was not a separate mountain, and the ridge dipped negligibly in between. Heading onwards, the ridgeline narrowed to a sharp apex with a 60-degree snow slope dropping 1,500ft [450m] on either side. This made for exciting climbing, and luckily clear skies and low winds cooperated. After only two close calls with crevasses near the summit, Dale and I achieved yet another first ascent of a virgin peak at 1700h on 25 August. This one measured 21,500ft [6,500m] even on the GPS, and constituted a broad east–west snow ridge which was reached via the south off Lefty Ridge.
>
> From the summit a third team member could be seen approaching along Lefty Ridge. Descending to meet the mystery member, Dale and Randall discovered that Gerard had been

(L–r): Annie Starkey, Ben Williams and Ger on the summit of a mountain in the Dahongliutan Range, China.

following their tracks all along the ridge. After sharing water and stories, it was discovered that Gerard had started at Base Camp at 0930h in the morning, and had already climbed 6,000ft [1,800m] in under eight hours! Gerard continued to the summit, and reached it at 1800h, to fly his Irish flag before a quick glissade back down.

The following is another account from Randall Krantz, this time of one of the last days in China.

There was a final welcome from our crew, including the last of the firecrackers and yet another huge lunch. We were cutting it close on potatoes, and Gin Gong threatened to go to Dahongliutan to buy more, despite some 20kg of pasta being left. Between washing clothes and ourselves, we have managed to find time to learn hurling tips from Gerard, who brought four hurleys all the way to Base Camp. Chasing a sliotar through scree at 14,800ft [4,500m] is not easy, even after four weeks of acclimatising!

This successful trip to China opened another door in Ger's life. His friend Annie had a house in Anchorage, and as the old house which Ger had been renting was in the process of being sold, he rented a room from Annie. She and Ger started dating later that year. Annie had a lot of the same interests as Ger, which helped to make them a dynamic couple.

When Ger arrived back in Alaska, he had an eight-month break in his contract with Glacier Software Inc. Having such a keen interest in nature he decided to take up a temporary job as a database administrator with a company in Anchorage called LGL. The company was involved in tagging beluga whales, and knowing Ger's love of the outdoor life, the tagging parties sometimes invited him along, to his great delight.

All-Irish Team on Denali

The following year, 2005, Ger set out to climb Denali again but this time with an all-Irish team. John Dowd remembers his second attempt to climb the mountain and how Ger was instrumental in making it possible.

I was there to climb Mount McKinley [Denali] with four others, and due to his cheerful nature it did not take long to get to know Ger.

This was my second attempt on Denali and it is the mountain that stands out in my mind as the most enjoyable that I have

Ger on Denali in 2005.

climbed so far. We were all Irish and had the best storyteller one could find in Ireland, Limerick man John Roche, coupled with the charismatic Ger; we were constantly laughing.

I was very fortunate to be on the same rope with Ger – the camaraderie, the sense of friendship made climbing so easy for me. Ger had the art of uniting teams; this gives one great strength, both emotionally and practically. Getting to the top of a high mountain is not important – sure, it would be nice, but what is important is friendship and teamwork.

This time I was fortunate to summit. I have Ger to thank for that, for the way he took our expedition under his control, making sure we had adequate supplies and motivating the team. From Ger I learned the importance of being patient on a mountain and identifying when to push forward, waiting for the right moment. I owe the success of that climb to Ger and my other team members.

I will never forget the long march down from high camp, it took twenty-one hours to reach base. Ger and I ran out of water halfway down the glacier and after arriving late in the evening we pleaded with the ranger to send a pickup plane. To our delight they agreed to send a plane and we were off the glacier up in the air when we saw our fellow teammates making their victorious march down the glacier. It was a lovely finish to what was a hard but enjoyable expedition.

The Irish team on Denali (*l–r*): Pat Falvey,
John Dowd, Clare O'Leary, Ger and John Roche.

9. FINAL SUMMIT MEETING (AND K2 2006 AND THE DECISION TO RETURN)

Summit Meeting Decision, 25 July 2008

On 25 July 2008 Ger and his fellow climbers on K2 got word that the weather for 1 August would be good. They would start their first joint bid the day before, thus giving the lead party a time and weather window if there were any delays. The weather forecast also suggested the days following the summit bid would allow a safe descent.

The Korean team had originally wanted to use 31 July to reach Camp 4 but had been convinced that the weather conditions would allow them to reach there on 30 July, clearing the way for a joint summit bid on 31 July and 1 August. Spirits were now high in the camp and climbers joked in their planning meeting that the next meeting would be in Camp 4, from which the summit bid would be launched. Those climbing the two alternative routes to the summit would meet in Camp 4 below the Bottleneck on 30 July, and the next day they hoped to start the climb to the summit. Posting in a blog from the K2 Base Camp to friends and family around the world, Ger let them know that a summit bid now looked a real possibility. '*Sin é anois, a cháirde*,' he said. '*Tá an t-ám ag teacht*.' ('That's it now, my friends. The time is coming.')

At last Ger was on the cusp of his dream to scale the summit of K2.

K2 and Broad Peak, 2006

Two years earlier Ger had first set out on an expedition to climb the mountain, one that almost ended tragically for him. Ger had first started to think about

Facing page: Leaving Concordia for Broad Peak Base Camp, 2006. (Courtesy Con Collins)

K2 viewed from Broad Peak Base Camp. (Courtesy Con Collins)

K2 after his success on Everest. 'I think there are a lot of mountains more interesting than Everest. K2 was one such mountain, and in 2006 I attempted it with an international team.'

Initially Ger had intended a low-key attempt on the mountain, but the reality of modern-day climbing on the major peaks is not so straightforward. 'I had planned on going out there and keeping it all low key but once I started my plans I tried to hire the facilitating company directly myself but they told me I couldn't and that I'd have go through a company called FTA. I guess they were somehow affiliated with Field Touring Alpine from Australia. I spoke with them and they asked me to send on my climbing résumé and they would review it. They accepted me as a member, so that summer we set off to climb both Broad Peak and K2.'

Ger had spent two years preparing for an attempt on K2 but it was through the suggestion of an Alaskan friend, Rory Stark, who had climbed on both mountains, that the idea of using Broad Peak as an acclimatisation for K2 came about. While Broad Peak was not a very technical (i.e. difficult, demanding a good knowledge of ropes and other equipment) climb, acclimatising there meant Ger would have to spend less time on K2, thus increasing the safety margin.

Ger climbing on Broad Peak in 2006.

Base Camp for Broad Peak was at 4,800m/15,700ft, compared to 5,000m/16,400ft for K2. The summit on Broad Peak was at 8,051m/26,414ft. K2 stood at 8,611m/28,251ft. Camp 4 on K2, from which the final summit attempt was to be made, through the Bottleneck, was 500m/1,650ft higher than the similar Camp 4 on the less dangerous Broad Peak. The only reason Ger had set out to go to Broad Peak was to achieve his goal of reaching the summit of K2. When he was accepted by FTA he had no idea who he would be climbing with but he need not have worried. Along with some fellow Irish climbers he would make great friends on this expedition and climb for the first time with teammates who would join him on his successful attempt on the summit of K2 two years later.

> I didn't really know who else was on the team at that point, it was only later that I came to find out that Mick Murphy was on it also. Then John Roche, Con Collins and John Dowd joined for Broad Peak. Mick Murphy and I had signed up for both Broad Peak and K2. With a team as large as twenty-two or so, naturally it broke up into groups. Ryan and J. J., the team leaders, were already acclimatised, from Everest no less, so it made sense that they pair up. Other groupings just happened based on climbing styles or personal goals. Wilco van Rooijen and I seemed to be more together on that score, so we pretty much climbed together for the rest of the expedition. Getting to climb any mountain with good people is always a wonderful thing. We'd a large international team and surprisingly enough we all got along famously. It was probably the biggest team that any of us was in so I suppose there were some growing pains, and some mental adjustments going on initially. We'd a couple of lads in the team that were great entertainers. The likes of John Roche from County Limerick really added to the laughs we had along the way. You can't have a bad day with them around.

The climb was an unguided expedition with FTA, who acted as a liaison with the local facilitating company, Alpine Trekking Pakistan (ATP), who, in turn, organised the permits, transport, porters, cooks and Base Camp. As with Ger's successful summit expedition in 2008 the team initially arrived in Islamabad followed by, in Ger's case, an earlier-than-scheduled bus journey to Skardu. Ger was eager to move on as the high level of pollution caused an adverse reaction with his asthma. The clear air of the high mountains meant that his asthma was not a problem when climbing, but the contrasting environment of

Pakistan's capital was not a pleasant experience for him. In Skardu the Irish members of the team, who had supportively left Islamabad with Ger, waited for the rest of the international team to arrive.

It was in Skardu that Ger met Mark Sheen for the first time. (Mark would later form part of the K2 team in 2008.) Ger said: 'I took an instant liking to him, as did my friend Dave Hancock who met him at the same time. He was friendly, considerate and spoke gently. He also seemed to really care about us when we first met. He seemed such a genuine character after only a few minutes. Upon walking into Base Camp it became clear to me that I wanted to be friends with this guy.'

From Skardu a fleet of Land Cruisers brought them to Askole. They were relieved to be trekking and climbing once again after the heat of the lower altitudes, escaping the monotony of the long and necessary travel to reach the mountains. The early part of the journey went without much of a hitch, with the exception that two of the international team were travelling without their gear; sorting spares was easier for some while they awaited delivery at Base Camp, as Ger recorded in his log:

> Well, some people's luggage was lagging behind due to problems varying from customs issues to the typical airline screw-ups. So a bit of drama there. Not very reassuring when you're told day after day that your gear will arrive soon only to have a no-show, day after day. I think the Swiss girl Joelle and the Ozzie giant Nick had to wait for a few weeks before their gear showed at Base Camp. Joelle could at least borrow gear that would fit her in the meantime. Nick on the other hand was just too damn big. I think while trekking in we had to virtually sprint to keep up with his brisk stroll. The man was massive. So there were no spare climbing boots that would fit him. His were special ordered. Not too sure what size shoe he takes. Some big-ass size. [Joelle Brupbacher was an accomplished climber and, after meeting Ger in 2006, had kept in contact with him. On the night of 22 May 2011 after reaching the summit of Makalu, Joelle died in her tent at high camp from exhaustion. She was thirty-three.]

An unfortunate accident in Camp 4 on Broad Peak cost Ger his first summit attempt on the mountain, as he recalled:

> Wilco and myself had a bit of an incident on our first attempt. We were in Camp 4 in two separate single-wall – read 'small' – tents

that were facing each other. Wilco had a stove running in his and he was about to pass me a second stove that had been cached in that tent. He decided to first screw on a gas canister to it. The canister had some ice on its threads, however, so it wouldn't make a perfect seal. He tried to force it but in doing so the gas shot onto the naked flame of the burning stove and wooosh, I just saw a huge ball of flame illuminate the entire tent. It all happened so quickly after that. I was sure Wilco would be seriously burned but he somehow managed to escape. He threw everything he could get his hands on towards the stove while simultaneously escaping from the inferno. From outside the tent he managed to contain it pretty quickly but not without burning a lot of gear and melting every sort of material onto the stove – neoprene, plastic, etc. I couldn't believe that he was absolutely fine, the tent too despite some charred bits here and there. But structurally it was sound, a lot sounder than the three-season piece of non-mentionable that I was in. We still had to make water at that point and I got the stove with gobs of industrial material melted onto it. We each retired to our tents and began to brew water. I tried to clean the stove as good as possible but nonetheless it wasn't long before the remnants of all that melted material turned my tent into a hazardous waste site. The burning fumes that came from the stove while trying to make water made me more and more nauseated until finally in the middle of the night I just couldn't keep anything down. Not even water. The following morning was just awash; there was no way I could make a summit attempt so down I went. The vomiting continued all the way to Base Camp. I could still smell the plastic in my nostrils the following day. That's the day that the other lads went for the summit. While Wilco and I were at Camp 4, Mick Murphy, John Dowd and Markus were at Camp 3. We came down from our botched summit attempt and they went up afterwards. There was a lot of tent exchanging like that going on throughout the expedition.

Having recovered from their accident, Ger and Wilco, along with Mark Sheen, made their second attempt on Broad Peak. Again things were not to go smoothly.

I arrived at Camp 4 only to see the two tents completely buried. After some digging it was apparent that one of the tents was badly torn and had a broken pole – not very good when only two poles hold it up anyway. We splinted the pole with a plastic knife and duct tape. What would we do without duct tape? Wilco and Sheen went into the other tent and I crawled into the misshapen excuse of a shelter but it was fine, really. It did the job, although it made for a fairly uncomfortable night as the warped pole would flip out of place and the entire tent would almost collapse while I was trying to brew water – with a clean stove this time. The plan was to leave at 3 a.m. and so we did. All except Sheen, that is. He didn't feel up to the job at the time.

The climb was over for Mark Sheen but Ger made a powerful impression on him during this expedition, so much so that they remained close friends and would once again team up for the climb on K2 in 2008. Mark recalls:

There were two personal experiences with Ger on this expedition which, I think, begin to define him. Firstly Ger and I went up to the first camp on an acclimatisation trip. We were to sleep in one of the new Eureka tents supplied on the expedition. There was only one tent for us to sleep in and upon arrival it became clear that this tent was way too small for both of us to sleep in. But we had to, there was no choice really. Not only was it too small but it was also perched on the side of a loose rock slope with an enormous drop behind the tent. The inside of the tent was also on much more of an angle than normal and there wasn't much you could do about it as the snow had melted underneath the tent to expose loose rock which couldn't be levelled. When I crawled in after Ger I couldn't help but just roll on him, because of the sloping tent, as I was on the upper side and the tent was so small anyway. Living in tents on mountains is always a cramped experience but this was seriously cramped and seriously out of shape. We could have got upset about it but not with Ger. Instead we laughed about our situation and talked of various ways to effectively 'kill' the tent and then send it off the cliff behind in flames once we had finished with it. We just laughed and joked. We must have sounded like a pair of drunkards because we were laughing about everything in the end, turning a terribly uncomfortable night into some kind of joyous occasion. Thank God for Ger's sense of humour that night.

Another night also sticks out. Towards the end of the expedition I suffered worrying levels of cold in one of my hands and feet on the way down from the mountain. I stayed alone in a tent trying to warm myself up during the freezing night. The next morning I was still cold and called out if someone could come over and help me with this. Everyone was exhausted, cold and wanted to go down as soon as possible. Ger was the one who came over and into my tent and clutched my foot close to his chest and under his jacket and stayed with me for at least an hour until my foot was warm enough to put back into my boot and make my way down. We were still over 7,000m [23,000ft] up the mountain and rather than just heading down as fast as he could, he stayed to make sure I was all right in circumstances which were very difficult.

Prior to helping Mark Sheen, Ger and Wilco had made a final push for the summit on Broad Peak, as recorded in Ger's log.

A lot more snow had fallen since our last attempt and we were soon wading chest deep in snow at times. It was just way too much work for two climbers at that altitude. So after a couple of hours we returned to Camp 4. At 7.30 a.m. we set off, knowing that we'd have to turn around before we reached the true summit. Typically the route veers climbers left into something of a snow bowl that leads up the gully that gains the ridge. Because of all the extra snow we decided to try and stay on the steeper stuff – 300m [1,000ft] perhaps of solid snow to grade three Alaskan ice. It was a sheer delight to get on it and it cut the drudgery of ploughing through deep snow significantly.

It was an absolutely marvellous day. The sights from the ridge-line were spectacular. China looked very red, I thought, no pun intended. Wilco and myself continued on and arrived at the false summit at 1 p.m. As expected we didn't have enough time to safely reach the true summit – two hours' round trip from the false summit. So we descended.

Ger and Wilco had failed to make the summit, but the climb to the false summit was more than enough for their acclimatisation for the real goal of reaching the summit of K2. Ger knew the risks of trying to take on too much and they had challenged their bodies to the limit. To go beyond and try to reach the summit outside the time frame recommended came with grave risks. Tragedy on the same mountain that day sadly illustrated the point to Ger only too well. At Camp 4 they encountered an Austrian team that was also heading for the summit.

> At Camp 4 we had noticed headlights coming from Camp 3 – a long stream of headlights. It was the Austrian team. We thought to wait a few hours and team up with them. It took them a long time before they arrived at Camp 4, however, way too late to safely make the summit – 7.30 a.m. But we set off nonetheless knowing that we'd have to turn around before we reached the true summit. The Austrians continued even though they were climbing much slower than Wilco and myself at that point. After all, their summit day started from Camp 3 while we started from Camp 4. I sat and spoke with their team leader, Markus Kronthaler, for a very short while. I just mentioned to him that Wilco and I had turned because we thought there wasn't enough time to reach the true summit. He didn't seem too pleased with what I was saying so I didn't say much else really. Later some of his teammates would summit as late as 6 p.m. He himself and a friend didn't make it to the summit that night and bivouacked between the false summit and the true summit. The following morning they summited.

On the way back down Kronthaler and his climbing partner got into trouble and sent out a distress call. Ger, now back in Base Camp, was exhausted along with the rest of the returning climbers. John Dowd remembers the situation in Base Camp at that time.

> There were two climbers from another team in trouble up on the summit ridge. Ger had met them on the ridge the day before on his way down from his second attempt and told them that it was late in the day, they were going too slow and advised them to turn around. However, they decided to push on, and twenty-four hours later they were making their way back from the summit when they sent out a distress call as one of them was in serious trouble and needed urgent help.

That evening all our team was back in Base Camp, exhausted after the climb, and our high-altitude sherpas were already in K2 Base Camp. Upon hearing about the distress call, Ger tried to get a team together by rallying around the base camp through the different teams.

I had never seen Ger so upset; he had tried everything possible, including negotiating with the distressed climbers' own team. Unfortunately, there was nothing that could be done that night. Next day the distressed climbers' own team put a rescue team together but it was too late – one climber [Kronthaler] had perished on the ridge.

For Ger, leaving them on the mountain, regardless of the life-threatening risk to any climber ascending at that stage, was something he found very hard to accept. Ger knew he could not make the rescue alone and, even with the support of fellow exhausted climbers, the chance of success without further fatalities was very low. In his notes on the incident he recalled Kronthaler. 'The following morning they summited but he lay down in their previous bivvy spot and died from exhaustion in the arms of his climbing partner. We were below in Base Camp at that point – helpless.'

10. STORM AT CAMP 3
(AND INJURY AT K2, 2006)

On 30 July 2008 Ger and his fellow climbers were up in Camp 3 on K2 at 7,350m/24,114ft as planned. The day had been fine, with hardly any clouds, and the wind was expected to lessen. The trek from Camp 2 had gone well, the climbers taking around seven hours to ascend just under a kilometre (half a mile) in altitude between the two camps, going at a slow and steady pace. That night the weather changed for the worse and for one climber, Serbian Hoselito Bite, near disaster developed on the edge of the mountain, as he relates:

> The day was beautiful and really nothing to indicate that the weather would change for the worse. I'm coming into Camp 3 at about 4 p.m. My tent is buried halfway, so I retrieved my snow shovel from my backpack and started digging. When I unearthed a proper base, I decided to move to a more comfortable place where Frenchman Hugues' tent was, which would later show that it was a big mistake. I entered the tent and was sipping melted ice. Outside the wind really started to pick up; after two hours the wind got stronger and stronger and it started to give me major problems with the tent. The snow was building up on the side wall, filling that space, with the tent slowly sliding towards the abyss … It turned out that the wind speed was around 100km/60 miles per hour and I could not control the situation. I stayed in my tent for hours but the snow and the wind smashed the tent. One moment the wind is blowing the tent, a huge tear rips along the tent, lifts the tent, and at that moment I throw myself on the left side of the tent towards the

wall but you still could not prevent the wind from pushing my tent to the abyss. I began to prepare for the worst situation that I will be forced to leave the tent. One moment the wind suddenly stopped and I thought that the weather calmed down. I let the bar of the tent down and started to melt ice again. The next moment a burst of wind began to blow and shot me back to the anchor of the tent and I was caught up in half the tent. I tried to raise the bar and set up the tent but the wind was so strong that I failed to do it. The tent was now leaning towards the abyss and I took the time to put a camera around my neck, belt, oxygen mask and feathered down suit. It was now time to leave the tent or if I'd stayed I'd have been blown down the 2,000m/6,500ft gully.

Outside the tent I immediately shouted to Gerard that I needed help. Gerard left his tent, broke the bars of my tent and helped me. He lit a light in his tent. I could see him in the dark and he yelled to me to come to another entrance as the wind was blowing directly at their tent and the open wind would blow it away. I quickly took my vacuum bag and a jacket I had with me. Things were so bad I did not even notice when I dropped the feathery jacket in the snow. I yelled to them, 'Quickly, open the door quickly!' Fierce gusts of wind smashed me in the face so hard that I could not open my mouth and breathe regularly. Pemba opened the door and I was petrified and totally as white as snow and stiff as a statue standing at the entrance of the tent. Pemba at the same moment grabbed me from the entrance of the tent and pulled me in along with tons of snow on me. I was lying in their tent and shaking due to the extreme weather while Pemba helped me take off my shoes and Gerard covered me with a bag. Pemba gave me hot water to drink and I soon began to feel better. I fell asleep after that. It was still relentless wind and snow on the tent – a two-man tent in which there were now four of us [Pemba, Ger, Jelle and Hoselito]. In the morning the wind was still hitting the tent while Pemba established radio contact with climbers who had been on the Abruzzi ridge, to see what the situation was.

Leaving the tent I saw the place where my tent had been; there was nothing more than a few parts left. The spot was almost completely buried with snow and if I had not been able to spend the night with Gerard in his tent I am quite sure that I would had been pushed down the slope with my tent and killed. Gerard saw my feathered sleeve jacket that I had dropped when leaving my tent the previous night. He proposed that we look for other parts of my equipment and perhaps even manage to continue to ascend. 'No, Gerard,' I told him. 'I lost some very important pieces of equipment and I am sure I will not survive the ascent. It kills me to say it but, my friend, I have to give up.'

When Ger and Pemba took Hoselito Bite into their tent, they had saved his life, and Bite watched sadly as they started up the mountain to Camp 4. The weather, as predicted, changed again to blue skies, boding well for their final summit attempt.

Setbacks During Ger's 2006 K2 Summit Bid
Ger was no stranger to setbacks during summit attempts on K2. Two years earlier his first summit attempt had been hit by serious problems, as he recalled in an interview with West Limerick 102 local radio.

> The first summit bid on K2 we all got stomach viruses. Initially a few lads got it but once I was in Camp 3 I got it as well. I was all roped and I started vomiting just as we were due to go for Camp 4. So whatever it was, we all got it. Certainly altitude played a role, no

The Abruzzi Spur on K2. (Courtesy ExplorersWeb)

Joelle Brupbacher and Ger (with head bandaged) after his accident in 2006.

doubt about that – definitely some viral thing going on. It wasn't your average run-of-the-mill bug as we couldn't even keep water down. We decided to head off again thinking that once our heart rates picked up we'd start to feel better. But it wasn't to be, so we all turned around.

We headed back to Base Camp and the plan was to go back up again. I had left some high-altitude gear in Camp 3 but when we tried to go back up again it was a little warmer, and while we slept at the Advance Base Camp the mountain was rumbling all through the night, just rock fall after rock fall. Looking back now I guess we should have listened to the mountain and did what it told us to do! The following morning you would set off in the darkness of early daybreak, the idea being that you'd minimise the amount of rock fall. Theoretically speaking, the avalanches don't fall as much in the cold of morning. We made it to Camp 1 safely. Wilco, a Dutch climber, and I had teamed up together, and there were another two Irish men en route: Mick Murphy and Banjo Bannon. Both had teamed up with American Ryan Waters, so we arrived in Camp 1 to melt some ice for water while we were waiting for them to come up. There was one other teammate there in Camp 1, a Swiss lady called Joelle who had arrived the previous day. While we were boiling water there were stones coming down like a bowling alley and we were the skittles. She was on lookout and would shout 'Watch out! Duck!' We'd retreat and get shelter to protect ourselves. We had finished preparing the water and Mick and Banjo had arrived so we decided to carry on. I was getting my gear together and then I set off and Joelle set off after me. Wilco was ahead of us on the open snow slope. What happened next I don't recall, nor anything of the previous two days. I was told about it afterwards.

Apparently Banjo and Mick roared up 'Avalanche!' I guess there was nowhere for me to go so I just ducked down and hugged the ground the best I could, hoping the rocks would miss me. They all did bar one, which met me on the helmet. If it wasn't for the helmet I'd be dead; even with the helmet I ended up with multiple fractures, a 5-mm dent in my head and a few hairline fractures running from the base of my skull to my forehead. Apparently at this point I climbed down to Joelle who was under me and, with my head and face covered in blood, said to her, 'Joelle, I think I'm bleeding!' I was serious and I was confused. We immediately went down to Camp 1 where Mick and Banjo were. They patched me up by taking off the helmet. There was a concern as to whether or not the helmet should be removed, but in the middle of the debate I just whipped it off. They packed my wound with socks to soak up the blood; you know you don't need much of a cut on your head to cause a lot of blood. The lads helped me down and apparently I started getting more confused as we were moving down from Camp 1. Banjo had me tied in, he had me short-roped between me and him and we abseiled down together, me staying pretty much as close as I possibly could to him. Thankfully we made it back to Base Camp with some of the Russians and Japanese that we had met at Advance Base Camp.

When something like this happens everyone pools together and there's a lot of team work involved. My first memory of that evening was sitting down watching *The Dukes of Hazzard* in Russian with no subtitles. I was looking around the tent and all I could see were Russians. I was wondering what the hell had just happened. What was going on? One Russian turned to me and handed me a sweet: it was so surreal. My next memory is waking up late that night in my own tent with Mick Murphy beside me. I'm certainly aware by now of the pain in my head. I wake Mick up and ask him, 'What has happened to me?' so he sits me down and explains and explains, and by morning it started to sink in. The helicopter was coming in late that morning and I was feeling OK. The record function in my head was starting to work again and I was packing my own gear at this point. As we waited I remember saying to Mick, 'I hope you're not coming off the mountain on my account.' But he said, no, he'd had enough of the mountain, so I said, 'Fair enough' and we headed for the military base hospital in Skardu.

It was the scariest facility I had ever been in, but it *was* a hospital. It reminded me of something out of *M*A*S*H*, the TV show, especially the operating theatre.

Back in Ireland, news filtered through about Ger's accident. Ger's sister Denise was shopping in Limerick when she got the call and immediately returned home to find family members outside crying: no one knew the real situation and many thought Ger was dead. The family prayed as they waited by the phone. Thankfully, after what felt like days, the good news was received – Ger would be okay. And while the family breathed a sigh of relief, Ger was struggling to deal with the local doctors in Skardu.

First the Russian doctor told me on leaving K2 to have a CT scan done. But this request was ridiculed in Skardu; instead the outcome was an X-ray, the results of which showed everything was normal. I was shocked and said, 'It doesn't feel very normal.' The surgeon said, 'Look, we need to operate, the wound is dirty and we need to remove those field stitches.'

I was thinking then that what they needed to do could have been done under a local anaesthetic but I guess local anaesthetics are expensive and they probably didn't have it. They were going to put me under with a general, so the morning of the surgery they came into the room with what looked like a piece of paper torn from a copybook and it had something written in Urdu. They asked me to sign it, apparently giving them permission to operate on me under a general anaesthetic. I signed it.

A few hours later I remember they were wheeling me into the operating theatre after receiving my general. The surgeon at this point wasn't aware that I wasn't fully unconscious so they lifted me.

I'll never forget what the surgery looked like, visually anyhow. It looked like a slaughterhouse, for the want of a better word. All the equipment was dodgy looking and filthy and to make matters worse I was still wearing the same clothes that had been on me for the past two months. So they lifted me onto the table – it was an old cracked leather one. I didn't really begin to get worried until they started to strap both my arms and legs down! I immediately thought, 'God, this is going to hurt.' The anaesthetist was standing to my left-hand side, someone else was to my right and the surgeon was, of course, behind me at my head. The anaesthetist just started taunting me, mocking my request to have a CT scan done and he started saying stuff like 'So where are your friends now?'

I just couldn't believe it. Here I was with an anaesthetist who was trying to make me as uncomfortable as possible instead of the other way around. He definitely succeeded in getting to me. They started to operate on me and clean the wound. The pain was unbearable once they started touching the stitches at all. It was way too much for me to bear so I squirmed away as best I could.

Eventually I shouted, 'Look, stop the procedure!'

With that, the guy to the right of me said, 'But you've signed the form to allow us to operate on you under general anaesthetic.'

Even at this point I was thinking, 'Can anyone not see that I shouldn't be arguing if I'm under a general?' I told them again to stop the procedure and, with that, the anaesthetist just gave me another dose and I felt the most unusual sensation as I went under, like that feeling you get if you fall backwards.

I later learnt what they had used on me is recommended for use only on animals but they still use it in third world countries and it was used on Vietnam-type field emergencies.

As I felt myself slowly go under I couldn't help but feel completely vulnerable. When I woke a few hours later I was writhing in pain on the bed. The day nurse was gone and the night nurse hadn't arrived yet. But when she did, she set me up. Painkillers galore. The anaesthetist had the cheek to show his face again. I jumped out of bed and just pointed at the door. 'Out,' I said. He just looked at me condescendingly and said, 'I'd nothing to say to you anyway.'

No satisfaction. I spent most of that day trying to contact the outside world. I never felt so alone in all my life. I suppose the trauma of the accident, the disappointment and the anaesthetist of

Frankenstein was messing me up royally. I couldn't get through to Ireland and I couldn't get through to the hotel where the rest of the team was staying, except Wilco who was still on the mountain. They finally arrived late that night. I was still on the phone trying to get through to someone. I just burst into tears. Surprised myself. I didn't even know I was that close to tears. Embarrassed, I turned and walked into the ward and hopped on the bed, still sobbing. God, like a little girl. Our team's liaison officer was consoling me. 'No, no, don't cry. You climbed K2.' As if that had anything to do with anything. It made me laugh though.

It turned out that there was a religious holiday that day in Skardu and the roads were packed full of people praying. I told them about the anaesthetist. They couldn't believe it. The story was already starting to sound funny but at the time I wasn't seeing the funny side of it all.

That night I was sitting up in my bed. The nurse noticed and came over to me. 'Pain?' she asked. 'Yeah, pain,' I replied. So she went over to her cupboard and filled a syringe full of something, came back and injected me with it and with a knowing smile she says, 'OK, have good sleep.' I don't remember hitting the pillow but I'd imagine it wasn't too long after that.

The following day I got the hell out of there despite their wanting me to stay longer. The plan was to get better medical attention in Islamabad but actually I was more interested in getting it in Ireland.

A day later they tried to fly me from Skardu, but typical of the bad weather I ended up taking a bus. Only two hours south of Skardu on an 800km [500-mile] trek, all the roads were closed due to landslides, so I had to start walking. It took me in total two weeks to get back home to Ireland and in the middle of it all that was the whole Heathrow terrorist fiasco. I had to pinch myself when the plane landed in Shannon. I nearly cried.

I received medical attention straight away once I was in Ireland. They found out, not surprisingly, that all was not normal; I had multiple fractures but thankfully no brain damage. But the injuries don't matter. The world is a fairly gripping place, and as I said before, these extreme places are addictive.

Speaking to the press before his first attempt to reach the summit of K2, Ger was asked about the competition to become the first Irishman to reach its summit and why they were attempting to climb this most dangerous of mountains. Ger's reply gives an insight into his approach to climbing. 'K2 has a tremendous appeal to us. I'd like to think that we're not going to detract from the aesthetics of the climb by getting wrapped up in a race to become the first Irishman to its summit. I'm just there for the climb. Competition would just fuel bad decisions on the mountain and there's no place for those on K2 or any mountain for that matter. Plenty of room for good times with friends, though. We're all looking forward to it.'

As he showed on Broad Peak and on numerous climbs before, Ger did not believe in reaching the summit at any cost. Things went wrong on the highest mountains that were often hard to explain – an unlucky rock fall on K2, for example – but making the right decisions for the right reasons was equally important. He would reach the summit of K2 two years later, but being the first Irishman to do so was not the driving reason behind his attempt.

Soon after he returned home Ger posted a message on his blog to all those who had been worried about him after the accident.

Thanks everyone for your well wishes. I'm recovering nicely all right here in Ireland. Unfortunately I can't tell you a whole lot about the accident, only what Joelle and Mick told me about it afterwards. The details of the day and the two days before are slowly returning though. Mostly the funny parts. Thankfully neither Mick, Wilco, Joelle, Banjo nor Jackcek were in the path of the rock avalanche. Wilco was above, Joelle was closest to me in a rock section before the snow field I was on and Mick and Banjo below in Camp 1. I'm not too sure where Jackcek was – either at Camp 1 or about to arrive there. For the descent it seems like I was merely operating in the present tense as I've no recollection of it yet, and yet according to Mick I was descending unassisted.

The Russians and Japanese then met us, Banjo, Mick and myself, at ABC [Advance Base Camp] and accompanied me back to Base Camp. I'm extremely grateful to a lot of people involved here of course – too numerous to mention. Also I have to say that Field Touring Alpine and Alpine Trekking Pakistan [the facilitating companies who had organised the trip] were extraordinary in their handling of the incident. Thank you. Sorry to have given all my friends a scare though. One thing's for sure, next time I'll have a sat phone of my own. I would have been able to alleviate a lot of the worry at home with one simple phone call.

Finally had a CT scan. Irish lads say they were mad in Pakistan not to give me one. Surprise surprise. 5mm depression fracture on one side and a minor fracture that runs along the base of the skull on the other. Heading to another hospital tomorrow where they are likely to operate – stick in a screw and pull it out. They might decide not to, due to the time elapsed since the accident.

Asked on his return from K2 in 2006 if he had plans to return, Ger had no doubts. 'Yes, I hope to head back to K2 again. Other mountains? Intentions yes. Plans no.'

11. BEYOND ENDURANCE (AND A CUP OF TEA ON DENALI)

It was clear to all that while Ger was interested in other adventures, to him K2 was one summit he was determined to reach. In the meantime, after a full recovery he had the opportunity to travel with some of the team from his Everest expedition. The destination was Antarctica, a place that had a special appeal for Ger. In 2003 he had been heading for Antarctica when the expedition was cancelled, giving him the chance to take up the invitation to climb Everest. Now Pat Falvey planned a groundbreaking Antarctic expedition, retracing the footsteps of Ernest Shackleton and Tom Crean. The expedition was called Beyond Endurance. The primary objective was to record the crossing of South Georgia, with an Irish team from all over Ireland, in honour of Irish Antarctic explorers and adventurers.

Clare O'Leary, who had climbed with Ger on Everest and had since returned to become the first Irishwoman to reach the summit of Everest, was also on the expedition. So were two climbers Ger was meeting for the first time, Norwegians Rolf Bae and Cecilie Skog, with whom he would climb again on K2 in 2008.

The trip involved traversing some very diverse landscape; team member Marie O'Neill remembers one such day.

> Today I walked from Fortuna Bay to Stromness on South Georgia. When you say it quickly it sounds like nothing, but it was beyond anything I hoped to do on this Antarctic adventure. I walked in the footsteps of giants, thanks Ger for the footsteps, and was also helped every step of the way by Cliff [Reid], Red [Cabot] and Augustan [surname unknown], among others. This was the last

leg of the main traverse, commemorating the feat of Shackleton, Crean and Worsley. One of the highlights was sliding down the snow behind Ger, maybe 200ft [60m] in thirty seconds. There were a couple of accidental slides too; Ger and Red had to stop me taking the feet from under people in front. We passed nesting Gentoo penguins high above Stromness Bay, looking down on the station. And there was the Crean Lake, a frozen wonder in a surrounding wonderland of snow-clad peaks. We crossed shale, climbed down shale, and climbed up shale, and the same with the tussock grass. Then we crossed boggy ground near the end when we arrived at the abandoned whaling station in time for the group photograph. Finally, we braved the fur seals to board the Zodiacs and return to the MV *Ushuaia*. The fur seals seemed to form a guard of honour for the traversers, but were more inclined to sample the rest of us for lunch, so the paddles that the Antarpply [a travel operator of Antarctic cruises] team carried came in useful again.

Clare O'Leary was glad to be on an expedition with Ger again but she knew K2 was exerting a greater pull on him, even though the timing of his next attempt was somewhat brought forward by a failure to get sponsorship on another trip Pat Falvey was planning.

Ger was around to take part in some of the celebrations back in Ireland, but then returned to Alaska. I stayed in regular contact with him through emails and calls and a year later took a trip out to Alaska to climb, ski and hang out. I got to meet lots of his friends, went to watch his band and generally got a feel for the life that he loved out there. Every day we headed off to see somewhere, do something – he wasn't working at the time and he literally spent the week entertaining me. I was preparing for my second Everest expedition at the time and we went around to the local gear shops where he was on first-name terms with those working there. I will never forget Ger's company on that trip. He just couldn't have been more decent and it was that trip that really sealed our friendship. We met up any time he came back to Ireland after that and was a number one choice for teammate on any future expedition.

We climbed together on McKinley (Denali) in 2005 and then, in 2006, as part of the Beyond Endurance expedition, we went to the

Antarctic Peninsula on board an icebreaker. A smaller team crossed South Georgia. It was an enjoyable trip and a great opportunity to see the islands, but for some of us it just wasn't energetic enough and we were certainly looking forward to getting back on land and the freedom that that brings! We had lots of fun messing and joking with the Norwegians – Rolf, Sigurd and Bjorn. The trip was to have been in preparation for a South Pole expedition – in planning this, it was Ger, Pat and myself who were to have made up the team. Unfortunately funding was an issue and when we failed to get sponsorship, Ger decided to go back to K2. He had already attempted K2 in 2006 but a head injury due to rock fall forced him off the mountain.

I had met Ger on his return – I was fascinated by K2 and wanted to hear about each section of the climb and, of course, the accident. His eyes shone as he spoke about it and there was no question in my head but that he would return. The only question was when.

Ger receiving a typically enthusiastic reception from his niece and nephews.

In spite of the eighteen-hour journey, coming back to Ireland from Alaska was always exciting for Ger; meeting his loved ones was the highlight of the year. A trip in September 2007, however, was an unscheduled one. He was home for a very short few days to accompany his mother, Gertie, to Croke Park to see his beloved Limerick in the All-Ireland hurling final against Kilkenny. Ger was disappointed with the result but he was still on a high as it was the first time he had been able to travel home to Ireland to see his county in Croke Park. A person once described Ger as the guy who always saw the glass as half full even if it was well below the halfway mark, and this was a prime example. Kilkenny won by 2-19 to 1-15.

On his numerous trips back to Alaska, Ger would often be seen travelling through Shannon Airport with two of D. J. Daly's finest hurleys neatly packed away in his gear. Ger was always on hand to teach the Alaskans about all things Irish and the GAA. One time Ger was bringing a consignment of six hurleys to Alaska and on arrival he rang his mother. Consumed with laughter, he was almost unable to talk as he explained that when he opened his pack of hurleys he discovered that someone in the luggage department in Shannon had taken the time to write 'Up Clare' carefully on each one. Ger could always take a good joke.

A Cup of Tea on Denali

In early 2007 Ger was back working with Glacier Software Inc., a job that brought him to the most remote parts of Alaska, including Deadhorse and Prudhoe Bay in the north. These destinations require a plane ride out. But Ger loved extremes and he was happy. He was particularly happy this summer as his brother J. J. and his girlfriend Céren were making the trip out to see him. Ger, as usual, was the perfect host. During that year an Irish team travelled to Alaska to climb Denali. One of his Irish friends, Micheál O'Connell, remembers meeting Ger for the first time and Ger's trip to Base Camp to have a cup of tea with the Irish team.

> Before we met him, Ger McDonnell was for us a big hairy giant we used to see in summit photos in Pat Falvey's house. We first met him at Pat's lodge in 2006, shaven and consequently unrecognisable. His gentle and unassuming demeanour further disguised the connection with the mountain-topping yeti we had expected him to be. But Ger it was, on a trip home with Annie. We were going to Denali the following year, 2007, and we sounded Ger out for the climb. He might like a training run before heading to the

Himalayas. He didn't have enough time off work to come along, but since his friend Rolf and some of his other Dutch friends, as well as ourselves, were on the mountain, he said he'd see if we could meet up at some point.

Logistically difficult, one would think, since we'd be leaving for Base Camp before he even got off work. Not a problem for Ger. There we were, sitting out some bad weather at the 11,000ft [3,350m] camp when a big hairy giant stomps up through the blizzard with a big grin on his face. He had arrived in Talkeetna, flight into Base Camp organised, and gone in to get his climbing permit. They have a habit of asking you, for the record it seems, what your 'goal' is in climbing the mountain: cue emotional climbers talking endlessly about self-fulfilment and the like. Ger was more direct: 'To have a cup of tea at the 11,000ft camp' was his answer. They knew him well enough to realise he meant it.

There was then the problem of getting across the glacier travelling solo. In a team of two or three, your partners will – so the theory goes – be able to hold you if you step through a snow bridge and into a crevasse. Ger was on his own, but it takes more than that to stop a Kilcornan man in Alaska, especially one with a ladder. The idea was that Ger would fit between two rungs in the ladder and the length of the ladder, ahead and behind, would hold on either side of the crevasse. It didn't quite work out that way as Ger's shoulders were bigger than he thought. So off he went from Base Camp with a 20ft [6m] ladder hanging off his side. The looks on the faces of all at Base Camp have not been recorded.

True to his word, Ger had that cup of tea, spent a night at 11,000ft [3,350m] and skied back down the following morning. We will never forget the experience.

Ever the Joker

The year 2007 was not just one for climbing and a story Ger's cousin Mike McDonnell remembers well from that year illustrates Ger's great sense of humour, especially when it came to members of his family.

My parents were forty years married in July 2007. To celebrate said events my sister Mary and I arranged a dinner for them and aunts/ uncles in the Woodlands House Hotel, Adare. As per Noah's ark, two of each family on either side were invited. The guests included

Gertie and J. J.

Dinner went extremely well and the conversation and *craic* was flowing in spite of the record number of teetotallers gathered. My daughter Anna was just over six months old at the time and at her biggest public gathering since her christening. We left about 10.30 as she was totally exhausted. As we left, the majority of the cohort were still huddled around the table with the dessert trolley lying innocently in the corner of the room.

I went to work the next day, tired but happy at the night's events. A few minutes after my arrival a mail winged its merry way through cyberspace to my account. It read as follows:

From: The Woodlands House Hotel
Sent: 31 July 2007 09:10
To: Micheal McDonnell
Subject: The dessert bill

Dearest patron,
It has come to our attention that an unauthorised 45 euros worth of desserts were consumed from the display dessert tray after the bill was paid. You at least obliged us by leaving your email address. Thank you for that. Please contact us at your earliest convenience so we can arrange payment. 061- …
With regards,
Shauna Davis
Hotel Manager

This mail was also blind copied to J. J. and another cousin who attended but I wasn't aware of this at the time. I had a vague recollection of the dessert trolley and knew some of the individuals involved would not be averse to sampling from an assortment of delectable items. I rang my sister, who confirmed that the poor defenceless trolley had been ravaged around 11 p.m. by a motley crew bearing small spoons and big mouths. In the meantime J. J. had mailed, aghast at the situation as well, which added to my confusion.

Mary agreed to go to reception to sort out the situation. Following a quick conversation with a receptionist it was explained that the Woodlands would never charge for such an event and the patrons were more than welcome to second helpings. Once I received this news I started to think about what happened. It then occurred to me that the Woodlands didn't have my e-mail address either.

Just then, another mail pinged through to my account. It was the bould Ger admitting responsibility. I could almost see the large grin on his face across in Anchorage. It turned out that he spoke with his mother the night before and formed his cunning plan, which he put into practice at very short notice. He also mentioned that if I had rung the number I wouldn't have been connected with the hotel as expected but would have reached the Limerick Gay and Lesbian Society. I don't know if the desserts included Baked Alaska but Ger sure made a pudding out of me that day.

Ger rounded off 2007 with his annual trip to Ireland to visit family and friends. True to form, he hit Dublin and made it his business to catch a performance by Kíla, his favourite Irish trad rock band. Ger became one of the main reasons that Kíla ended up playing in Alaska. He loved the excitement of a Kíla gig and they never disappointed him. Colm Ó Snodaigh of Kíla remembers their Alaskan trip with fondness.

> … and so it came to pass, one day, that Kíla went to Alaska to play two concerts – all Ger's doing of course. When he set his mind on something he generally achieved it.
>
> We were at the tail end of a three-week tour and were a little tired after a long flight but Ger was full of chatter and enthusiasm and brought us straight to a bar, in the centre of Anchorage, whereupon we met a girl we knew from the Corca Dhuibhne Gaeltacht, Liadain Slattery (she was mates with Ger – he was mates with a lot of pretty women!).
>
> The first concert, in Anchorage, was full to the brim – 1,200 people buzzing with the music. Some of the crowd started dancing in the aisles and this freaked out one of the organisers who came on stage, grabbed a microphone and said that she was going to switch off the sound if people didn't sit down. We held our nerve and played the concert for Ger and his friends when our instinct was to let the organiser carry on with the entertaining on her own.

Ger had spent years trying to get us to come to Anchorage and we weren't going to mess up his night.

The following day we travelled to Fairbanks where we really began to feel the cold. Ger, of course, walked around after the show dripping with sweat, oblivious to the cold, in a T-shirt, while we all froze beneath several layers of clothing.

It was a great club and we were rocking out when suddenly a great big bra came up on stage striking Rónán on the head. We were all a little amazed but laughed it off as one of those odd occurrences – we aren't Joe Dolan or Tom Jones and so this kind of thing just doesn't happen to us.

A tune or so later and another giant bra arrived up between Brian and Lance. A second or so later an extra-large pair of frilly knickers was flung at us! And then another tune later a whole slew of knickers and bras came soaring onto the stage. It didn't make any sense to us. It didn't seem like a crowd of sex-crazed girls and none of the women present seemed to be undressing.

Later we found out that Ger had stopped off at the local Walmart, bought a load of over-sized bras and panties and handed them out to his friends to fling at us.

Since then we stayed in touch by email and also tried to catch up with each other whenever he was in Ireland. His passionate company was a pleasure and his mischievous smile a blessing. I remember a night in Dolan's in Limerick city when Ger danced his way around the crowd all night, bringing laughter and joy to everyone. He created the vibe that night – not us. He used to come to the Kíla Christmas shows every year and we would natter after the show about poetry, music, his next climbing exploit, Kíla's current projects and all of life's great mysteries.

I can't remember where I was when the news came through that he had conquered Everest and that he'd whacked a sliotar off the top of the world. I remember how proud I felt knowing him. I remember also being quite shocked when he told me later over a pint in Glasnevin's Gravediggers pub that it was too easy.

Shortly after he injured himself on his first attempt to climb K2, Kíla were playing in Ballybunnion, in a wet and windy car park at the shambolic, inaugural World Fleadh. On our journey home the following day we dropped in to Kilcornan to see if we could catch the man with the hole in his head. And joking aside, I realised then how dangerous a path he was following. It was then also when I realised that he grew up only 10 miles/16km from where I spent many a summer holiday at my granny's in Newcastle West. Later I wished I'd known him then so we could have played hurling or football together. I reckoned we would have made a fine centre midfield pairing!

The Christmas before his 2008 trip to K2 he came to the Tripod, to the Kíla Christmas show. I was very sick and left the venue straight away to go back to bed and so we didn't catch up. He left me a copy of a book he'd finished on the plane – *The Iceman*. We swapped texts and a couple of emails. I wished him luck on his forthcoming K2 escapade, followed his journey upwards and celebrated his magnificent achievement of summiting. I imagined him embracing the world on top of K2, smiling his radiant smile as if to cheer the whole world up and singing Rónán's 'Tine Lasta' in his quiet unobtrusive way to let the world know who he was, where he was from and who his people were.

I was, and still am, honoured to be one of his people.

A Talent for Friendship

On one of his many trips back to Alaska from Ireland Ger met and became friends with Nora Morgan, an American, who was not only impressed by his exploits but his passion for K2.

The first time I met Ger was on a flight from Shannon to Dublin to Chicago. I used to be a flight attendant for an American charter airline. My crew was returning from an international trip on Aer Lingus as passengers because the planes we fly were staying overseas. The first leg of the flight to Dublin was fairly empty. My seat was in the very back of the plane and there might have been only ten people in that section. I was celebrating the idea of having a whole row to myself when this tall, handsome man with a stellar smile made his way towards me. I can't remember which one of us spoke first but we both were happy about the opportunity to stretch out. Even though it wasn't my airline, I kicked into flight attendant mode, got him some pillows and blankets and put him in a row all for himself.

We landed in Dublin and the plane began to fill up. It was obvious that our good luck had ended and not only were there not going to be empty rows, there weren't going to be any empty seats. A harried-looking businessman in a rumpled suit came towards where I was sitting and put his briefcase in the overhead bin. The young man I had met earlier tapped him on the shoulder and asked the businessman if he was sitting next to me. When he confirmed this, the young man asked if he would mind switching. It was quite humorous as the businessman began to protest and get red in the face. The young man calmly said, 'No really, I want you to move. I want to sit there,' and the businessman instantly shut up and complied. I was impressed because I have seen some serious fights escalate on planes from simple requests such as these and he handled it with such grace. I was also flattered and excited because he looked much more interesting then the businessman. International flights can be excruciatingly long and boring with no one to talk to. As he moved into the seat next to me he introduced himself as Gerard McDonnell. Like most Americans, I struggled to pronounce it the right way.

We spent the next eight hours talking about everything you could imagine. Ger had a way about him that made me and everyone around him feel good. I may be generalising a bit here but the international flight attendants on Aer Lingus (not the ones that fly locally) often give a chilly reception to us American travellers. They don't seem to like us very much. When they come around and ask what you want to drink and they hear an American accent it is like this mask falls over their faces and their demeanours become polite but cold. Sitting next to Ger made the trip much better. It was like he could feel the change in the temperature so he put the flight attendant at ease. He started speaking to him in Irish and they started laughing. He had told the flight attendant that he was trying to teach his friend (me) Irish but I was a terrible student. What followed was the two of them trying to get me to say different phrases and me failing miserably. For the rest of the flight the flight attendants were friendly and warm. It was lovely.

The two of us talked about our lives, music, what we did for fun. Me travel, him climb. I did not know that much about climbing but it always looked fun. I asked him if he had a dream of climbing any particular mountain. He said K2 and I kind of looked at him funny. The only thing I knew about that mountain was a movie I saw about it once and that it was incredibly dangerous but we were talking about dreams so I just shrugged it off. Understand that he just said he climbed for fun. He seemed to have a love of life that was contagious. I told him about what I wanted to do with my life and the way he looked at my dreams made me question why I hadn't gone after them already. He was inspiring. He made me realise that I was the one in charge of my own life and that I had a responsibility to make it the best I possibly could.

He changed my life that day. It may seem crazy to say that one conversation can change someone's life but it is true. When I returned to my home, I googled his name and pages and pages came up. He never said anything about his previous accomplishments. I had never met someone so humble. He was a normal guy who had achieved extraordinary things. It made me think that I could do so much more with my own life. At the time, I was in an emotionally abusive relationship and I ended it immediately following that trip. I never told him that but he helped me to see the truth.

We stayed in touch and saw each other whenever the two of us were in Ireland at the same time and he was a pretty good tour guide. My little sister also lived in Alaska (Juneau, not Anchorage) and one time we were both there during the Alaska Folk Festival. He introduced me to his friends and his music.

Focus on K2
For his final push to get trained up for K2 the following year, Ger stuck to a serious regime.

Back to Basics:
1. Bed by 9 p.m., up at 5 a.m.
2. 5–6 a.m. Exercise with 30 mins cardio, 30 mins weights
3. Fruit only in the morning (2 portions)
4. Salad only at lunch (large portions)
5. Protein shake and vegetables only for dinner (small portions)
6. Exercise at 7 p.m., 45 mins cardio, 45 mins weights
7. Drink recommended amount of water per day – at least 64 oz/1.9 litres!

REASONS:
1. Decrease weight!
2. Increase speed of hiking
3. Increase speed, agility and efficiency of climbing
4. Feel healthier and more agile in everyday life
5. Light and fast – get to the summit of K2
6. Goal – 200lbs
7. K2 goal – SUMMIT!
Project – Get the hell to 200lbs
Knock off the ridiculous
Goal date 5/11/07
GO! YOU CAN DO IT!

During his time in Anchorage Ger took every opportunity to use the local resources as he had to continue practising his climbing. The Chugach mountain range was tested in 2007 and was a perfect training ground for Ger. He had K2 in his plans for the following year, something he would keep under wraps until everything was in place. He had spoken with some people regarding the climb, but few at home really knew about it. Mark Keenan, though, a close friend of Ger's, spoke to him about it.

> Ger mentioned to me that he definitely planned to go back to K2 the next summer and that he had started making arrangements. I was immediately aware of the possibilities of this and I asked Ger a bit more about it. His words made it clear that he was aware of the dangers involved, but that he was going back to the mountain. Part of me felt like trying to dissuade him from doing this – but I reasoned with myself that I had no right to tell Ger McDonnell, the man who had climbed Everest, what to do even though I counted him among my best friends. Ger had always seemed invincible, but in the following months I felt a distinct sense of unease about Ger going back to K2.

Status: Unknown

The Norit website was the only source of information on Ger's status since reaching the summit of K2; the family had not been contacted by anyone from Norit. 'Gerard McDonnell: UNKNOWN' was flagged on the computer screen for forty-eight hours. Calls were made from Ireland to Alaska and the Canaries (where Ger's brother J. J. was on holiday), but there was no more information to be had. Ger's family crowded around the computer screen; this was the only available contact with was happening to him. Prayers were said, tears were shed but hopes remained high. Thousands all over the world watched the same screen and waited. The Norit website got so many hits that weekend it crashed several times.

Later on the evening of Saturday 2 August (Irish time), news filtered through that a lone climber had been spotted moving down somewhere between Camp 4 and Camp 3, apparently lost, but moving down. The McDonnell family were elated; they were sure it was Ger. Fingers were crossed and again prayers were said. It had to be Ger. This was a good sign and at last members of the family could sleep knowing good news was close. Ger's sister Denise had not slept since Friday morning. She monitored the computer all weekend. No member of the family was about to give up on Ger – his sister Stephanie even went to bed holding her phone so that she would not miss any calls about Ger.

The McDonnells had gone to bed with the hope that Ger would be located by morning. That hope was destroyed at 5.30 a.m. when I received a call from Pat Falvey to confirm that it was Wilco who had been spotted and that Ger was gone. I had to go and break the dreadful news to the family on the morning of 3 August.

My memory of those few days is as follows:

On the afternoon of Friday 1 August 2008 spirits were high and our hearts were filled with joy. Ger McDonnell had become the first Irishman to summit the 'savage mountain' known as K2. Ger always knew that after his experiences on K2 in 2006 he was capable of reaching its summit. At home the McDonnells knew that the job was only half done – celebrations wouldn't be started until Ger at least got to a safe camp.

For what felt like an eternity the family kept a vigil by both phone and Internet to see just how Ger was doing. That evening news broke that an accident had occurred on K2 and two climbers were dead. Details were very sketchy but again hopes were high that Ger would be accounted for shortly. For the next eighteen hours my wife, Denise, along with the family, stayed up and were focusing on the refresh button to update the Norit website and see if there were any changes, but all the time it read 'Gerard McDonnell: UNKNOWN'. Where was Ger and why hadn't anyone been able to tell us what was going on?

On Saturday morning I woke and went downstairs and could smell freshly brewed coffee coming from the kitchen. Denise was still hanging over the computer after having a long night, emailing her cousin Louisa Nash who had been helping Denise try to find answers, emailing Maarten, the Norit webmaster, who could give her nothing, and speaking with Ger's girlfriend Annie on the telephone. Denise looked to me and said something wasn't right, and with that she proceeded to call her mother, Gertie, and travel up to her sister Martha's house.

J. J. at this point was in Lanzarote on holiday but only two days previously had received an uplifting text from his brother to wish him happy birthday and say that they would be pushing for the summit shortly.

I remember sitting in the kitchen and I decided to call an old climbing pal of Ger's and possibly the only man I felt at that time who might be able to give us answers, Pat Falvey. Pat had, of course, also been keeping a close eye on what was happening out there. Along with Ger, Pat was also friends with Rolf Bae, a Norwegian who had been on Pat's 2007 Antarctic expedition and who was also on K2. He was delighted, he said, to help out the McDonnells in any way he could.

All that day the screen still read, 'Gerard McDonnell: UNKNOWN'. It's best described as being on a telephone with an automated machine and all you want to do is talk to someone. We weren't getting any correspondence from Norit. Maarten was bogged down with emails and queries, and to make matters worse, we were in Ireland, Maarten was in Holland and K2 was in Pakistan; it was hard and very frustrating for all involved. On the Saturday night we heard that Rolf, Ger's friend from Norway, had been killed by a serac avalanche and that Ger was with him. Thankfully the one person that really thought about the logistics of where everyone was on the mountain was Annie. She knew Ger couldn't have been with Rolf as Ger had summitted at approximately 6.30 p.m. and Rolf didn't, due to some difficulties he was having. It made it impossible for Ger to be with him.

Still the screen read, 'Gerard McDonnell: UNKNOWN'. Eventually more news filtered through from the mountain – a lone climber had been spotted. Again our spirits were raised because we knew that if anyone was strong enough to pull through this it was Ger.

Denise and her sisters Martha and Stephanie, along with their mother, Gertie, decided to get some sleep. It was now nearly 3 a.m. but thankfully we'd have good news in the morning … or so we thought. Martina, a friend of the family, had just gone home after making possibly her hundredth cup of tea that afternoon.

Martha and Barry's home that weekend had become our central hub for information, with friends and family calling to see if there had been any developments.

At about 5 a.m., Denise's cousin David O'Connor and I both travelled to my house a short distance away, as the Internet had crashed in the Lynch household. I received a call in my front room, one I'll never forget. It was Pat Falvey. I remarked to David that as it was past 5 a.m. it could only be news that Ger was dead or alive.

'Damien, you need to prepare the family for the worst,' he told me. I'll never forget the feeling of pure numbness. 'Ger is gone,' he continued. I put the phone down and David knew from my response that Ger was dead.

I phoned J. J., who was at the airport trying to get a flight home to Ireland to be with his family. I spoke with him and neither of us could contain ourselves. It was a terrible call both to make and receive, but I had promised J. J. that whatever happened I would keep him posted. Next was Annie; she had already received the news from Maarten and was devastated. What were we going to do?

I remember phoning Barry and Tom, Martha and Stephanie's husbands respectively. I told them the news and we arranged to meet in half an hour at Barry and Martha's house. Ita and Joanne, cousins and close friends of the McDonnells who had been at the house most of the weekend, went down to wake Denise. The last time she was woken to face death was when her father died; now her brother was gone. Barry and Ita drove down to tell Gertie and Stephanie. Gertie sat on her sofa. It was 7.45 on a Sunday morning, and every Sunday morning when Ger was on an expedition he would call the house at exactly eight o'clock. Gertie wasn't leaving the house until the phone call came, but it never did. She came up to the others and embraced them.

Within hours the press had got wind of what had happened and they started approaching locals going to Mass to ask them about Ger. Most of them didn't even know about the accident. It was suggested that the family release a press statement to keep the media at bay for the time being. Barry and I spoke with friends of ours who were involved with the press, Jerome and Clare O'Connell, and immediately they drove down from Ennis and organised everything. Speech and press meetings were sorted, so all I had to do was read out the statement.

'He brought honour, not only to us, his family, but the whole country, when he became the first Irishman to summit K2 on Friday.

'The last few days have been a roller coaster of emotions as we celebrated with joy his historic achievement, and now must try to come to terms with the untimely loss of a great son, brother and friend.

'Ger's love of mountain climbing was surpassed only by his love of family and friends. Our thoughts are with his girlfriend Annie in his adopted home of Alaska where he spent the last ten years. Above all we'll miss Ger's caring smile which brought light and warmth to all those who met him.

'He was a great son and brother, he had a great love of traditional Irish music and despite living away for the past number of years he was a true and proud Irishman. We would like to sympathise with the other families that lost a loved one on the unforgiving elements of K2 this past weekend – our thoughts and prayers are with them.

'We now ask the media for privacy as we come to terms with the news our beloved Ger will not be coming home to us. Thank you for your cooperation.'

It worked for a while, at least.

Later that evening, queues of people lined up outside to offer support and condolences to the McDonnell family. It was a remarkable sight and to make matters worse there was still no definite confirmation that Ger was gone. I suppose, if I was to be honest, I knew deep down that he was gone but just did not want to believe it. Annie arrived a day later and again it was very emotional for both her and the family to be coming into Ger's home without him.

On the Internet there were various stories as to how Ger died: he refused to come down; he went up towards the Chinese side of the mountain; he was out of his head and didn't know what he was doing. Something just wasn't adding up – how could so many different stories come off the same mountain regarding the same disaster? We needed to find out. I spoke with J. J. briefly; he wasn't happy with all the stories. On hearing that his brother could have headed up towards the Chinese side he immediately got in contact with Pakistani government officials, who assured us that they had scoured the mountain. Alarmingly, what we learned later was that when they say they'll scour the mountain they mean only their side of the mountain. China and Pakistan have a very delicate relationship and have strict policies regarding K2, with neither side allowed to fly in the restricted zones. J. J. then contacted the Irish government, who in turn got in touch with their Chinese counterparts. We had to leave no stone unturned. As J. J. said to me, 'If it was me out there, Ger would do all in his power to find me.'

It was decided we would travel to Pakistan and meet the climbers and try and collect Ger's gear.

12. FULL STORY AFTER K2 SUMMIT: DRAMA AT HOME

On the morning of 2 August several climbers were safe in Camp 4: Pemba and Cas from the Norit team, the Norwegians Cecilie and Lars, Kim Jae-soo, the leader of the Korean team and their star female climber Go Mi-sun, along with sherpas Chhiring Dorje, Pasang Bhote and Tsering Bhote. Cecilie's husband Rolf and the Frenchman Hugues were known to have perished in avalanches. Who was still at large on the mountain? Silently Pemba was doing his own head count. Eight people were still out there: Ger, Wilco, Marco, three Koreans with Sherpa Jumik Bhote, and Hugues' climbing companion, Karim Meherban, were still out there somewhere on the peak above Camp 4.

After reaching the summit of K2 on the evening of 1 August, Ger's spirits remained high. He and Marco Confortola were descending together, but their descent was slowed by a group of climbers further down on the ropes. Around midnight they could see four headlamps ahead of them, but suddenly, in the blink of an eye, all four disappeared. The implications of this did not immediately sink in, but when they realised this meant that four climbers had fallen, Ger and Marco decided that it was too dangerous to continue in the dark. They stopped for the night, digging shelter holes on the mountainside above the Traverse to sit it out until daylight. At this stage survival was the only thing on their minds. At above 8,000m/26,000ft on the mountain both experienced climbers knew that physically their bodies were starting to suffer due to the extreme altitude. Both were literally dying from the lack of oxygen at this altitude; if they didn't get down to a lower altitude soon they would die. Ger sang to Marco to try to keep their spirits high. Some hours later Wilco, making his way slowly down, spotted their headlamps and joined them. He

Marco Confortola (left) and Ger on the Traverse.

too decided to bivouac and wait for first light. Wilco recalls that the men said very little, but at Ger's request, he did try at one stage to see if he could find the correct route. 'He asked me to look again to find the correct route but my search was fruitless, we were stuck until daybreak.'

At first light on 2 August, Ger and his two fellow climbers got up and tried to get their bearings but at this point, because of the serac fall, nothing looked familiar to them. Wilco and Marco tried to decide which route was best to take, while Ger also tried to puzzle out where they were. Wilco became very impatient at this point; he suspected he was suffering the early signs of snow blindness and told his fellow climbers that he needed to descend quickly. They all started to descend but Wilco moved ahead of his companions, racing against time. At about 6.15 a.m. he turned a corner to see a sight that shocked him. Tangled on a fixed rope were two Koreans and Sherpa Jumik Bhote. All three men had made the summit. These were the headlights that Ger and Marco had seen disappear earlier in front of them. They had seen four headlights but there were only three men on the rope, which meant that one Korean climber had fallen to his death. These men were in a bad state and had been hanging upside down for the best part of three to four hours. The first

Korean climber was making deep moans of pain; his body and those of his companions were going through the stages of shutdown. The second Korean was silent and staring like a man who had given up. Jumik Bhote had lost a glove and a boot, so Wilco gave him his spare gloves. Wilco tried to talk to Jumik, but Jumik, who was carrying a radio, told him, 'Help is on the way.' Wilco understood and knew that his waiting around was not going to help anyone. Priority number one was his own safety, and priority number two was his wife Heleen and son Teun back home. Wilco started to descend again but he did not know that he was going the wrong way, heading too far to the west.

Meanwhile, Ger and Marco were slowly coming down the mountain in Wilco's tracks. Suddenly they were faced with the same shocking sight that Wilco had seen, three climbers tangled in ropes and left for dead. 'They were like puppets on a string,' said Confortola. 'When you straightened one guy the other twisted more.' Simply to cut the rope was impossible because of the 70-degree incline; if done it would mean certain death for the men. Whatever fears the men had to overcome in the dark the night before, now they felt compelled to stop and try to help the stranded climbers. According to Marco they spent three hours trying to comfort and disentangle the men. Marco decided he could do no more; he was exhausted and needed to get out of the death zone, and fast. To his surprise Ger did not descend with him. Instead he turned back and climbed back up towards the summit.

Ger's action at this point became a crucial point of contention among other climbers and commentators, and the various rumours caused major anguish to his family. Marco told reporters that 'McDonnell, perhaps confused by lack of oxygen, climbed back up the slope towards the summit'. In contrast, Nick Rice, who had been climbing with Hugues' expedition, and knew Ger well, wrote in his blog that 'Irishman Gerard McDonnell – confirmed dead – refused to descend because he was helping the others that were injured'.

Ger had a reputation as someone who could not leave another climber in distress, as had happened on Denali and again on Everest. On Broad Peak, despite the risks, he had tried to get together a rescue party for the stranded Austrian climbers, but his fellow climbers, knowing that it involved an unacceptable risk to their lives, refused to go. Ger had been devastated but knew a rescue attempt on his own had no chance of success. While on a climb in Alaska in early 2000, he came across a climber who had been cut off from his team and left for dead. This man had very serious injuries. Ger knelt down beside him, took out his rosary beads and prayed, staying with the dying man until he passed away.

On K2, despite his earlier concerns about the certain risk to his life by spending more time at high altitude, once again he was faced with fellow climbers in a life-threatening situation who needed his help. Ger knew from his rescue training, taken for his climbs on Denali, that if he could climb above the stranded climbers he could, by tying them to a different rope and transferring the load, free the three climbers. To do it he would need to reach the point above the climbers where the rope was fixed to an anchor and, having determined which rope within the tangle was loaded, clip a different section of rope to the existing anchor. Once that was done he could transfer the load to the untangled rope by cutting the loaded rope.

Why Ger turned back for the summit without telling Marco of his plans we will never know for sure. It is not easy to communicate at altitude in full climbing gear; perhaps he was intent on the job in hand, and saving energy. Maybe he was worried for his fellow climber, and did not want to lead him into taking an unacceptable risk by staying longer at high altitude. One of the sherpas said Marco was complaining of feeling weak at the summit the previous night. Whatever the reason, the fact is that Marco continued down the mountain. Making his way down through the Bottleneck, Marco heard a loud bang and looked up to see a climber whom he believed was Ger, because of his yellow boots, falling in an avalanche of ice and rock which smashed his body to bits. Marco then collapsed unconscious at the bottom of the Bottleneck. More than one authoritative commentator on the tragic events on K2 in 2008 has suggested that by this point Confortola's memory and perception (to the point of hallucination) could have been adversely affected by the long period spent at high altitude.

Pemba, taking a picture from Camp 4 at least an hour later, at 10 a.m., captured a climber above the three entangled climbers. While the detail of the photograph is merely dots, it is clear a rescue is taking place and, given the location of the climbers on the mountain, the man above the climbers could only have been Ger.

While all this was happening, down at Camp 4, Korean expedition leader Kim Jae-soo was urging the two sherpas in his team to climb back up the mountain. Three members of the Korean expedition were missing and its leader Kim knew that the longer they were out there, the less chance they had of survival. Kim wanted the sherpas Tsering Bhote and Pasang Bhote to go back up the mountain to rescue his missing expedition members.

The weather was beginning to turn and the Bottleneck was prone to serac falls and avalanches; it was extremely dangerous. Pemba, who had just been very sick from exhaustion, and was far more experienced than the Bhotes, tried to stop the Bhotes from going up but there were also family loyalties involved. Jumik Bhote, sherpa to the missing Koreans, who was trapped on a tangled line, was Tsering Bhote's elder brother and Pasang Bhote was his cousin, all from the same village in Nepal. Although both were suffering from exhaustion after spending most of the night at the shoulder, family loyalty demanded that they go back up to look for their relative. Pemba could understand that, but he was outraged that their boss, Kim, also expected them to rescue the three missing Koreans.

Around 11 a.m. when the Bhotes were on their way up, Pasang called Pemba on the radio and told him they had found a climber unconscious but still breathing, lying flat on his back at the foot of the Bottleneck. Pemba asked what colour the man's down suit was and from the answer he knew it was Marco. Going against his own advice, Pemba set out to rescue Marco, and at least try and search for his missing friends, Wilco and Ger. Pasang and Tsering continued up the mountain.

As Pemba ascended he could hear the rumbling of the mountain. 'It is not happy,' he thought. Avalanches were a serious threat now and what he was doing was possibly suicidal. After two hours Pemba finally reached the base of the Bottleneck where he found Marco lying flat on the snow, barely conscious. His downsuit was unzipped, gloves removed, boots open and his harness hanging. He pulled him up and started administering oxygen. As Marco came around, he struggled with Pemba and tried to refuse the oxygen, but for now at least his life was safe.

As Pemba was helping Marco, he received a second radio call from Pasang Bhote who reported that he had met with the Koreans and Jumik on their way down the mountain. Jumik and two Koreans had been freed from the ropes since Marco had left them. Pasang had met the climbers at the upper Bottleneck. His radio call confirmed that the team had been freed and made it across the Traverse. Pemba was disappointed to hear that neither Wilco nor Ger was with them, and asked Pasang if he had seen anyone else on the mountain. Pasang radioed back: 'No one else here, just Koreans and Jumik, but a few minutes ago I saw one person fall down from the Traverse section after being hit by a serac. I can't see him now as the visibility is extremely poor.' 'Could you identify the colours of his suit?' Pemba asked.

Pasang said he could: it was red with black patches. 'This to me was Gerard,' Pemba recalled later, 'because the Koreans didn't have a complete red down suit, Hugues didn't have a red suit and Karim had a pure red suit.' So while Marco had been mistaken in identifying the climber who fell past him while he was on the Bottleneck as Ger, Pemba knew now that his friend was gone. Having carried out the most extraordinary of rescues, Ger had been swept off the mountain by a falling serac, the same kind of ice fall that had taken the life of Rolf Bae the evening before.

The highly acclaimed website ExplorersWeb later pieced together the evidence of this stage of the climb, and confirmed Pemba's version of Ger's last moments. Pemba eventually also supplied photographic evidence to back it up, photographs he had taken with Ger's camera. All agreed that Marco's 'eyewitness' account was mistaken in the identity of the falling man with yellow boots.

> At this point, Marco believed that Gerard was dead. Towards the bottom of the Bottleneck, he had heard a loud bang and seen a waterfall of ice coming from the serac pinnacle 400m/1,300ft above. Marco said that he saw the three Koreans [*sic*] and 'Gerard's yellow shoes pass me'.
>
> A picture taken at the time however, at 10 a.m., showed the group of climbers still at the upper part of the Traverse, far from the top of the Bottleneck. For them to have slid all that way they would first have had to travel the long Traverse and then make a sharp turn down. In addition, about five hours later Pasang met up with them. Pasang called to Pemba at around 3 p.m. with the astonishing news. He said that the two Koreans and Jumik Sherpa were safe, they had some frostbite but were okay. 'Did you see anyone else?' enquired Pemba. 'There was a man in a red suit with black patches following close behind the three,' Pasang replied, 'but only a few minutes ago he was hit by a chunk of a serac and fell.' Pasang met the climbers at the start of the Bottleneck. His radio call showed that the team – avalanched, entangled and believed to be virtually dead – had been freed and made it to the Traverse.
>
> So where does that leave Marco's testimony? The same picture mentioned above, showing climbers far away from the serac, also showed a single person sitting above it. In another picture, shot later that evening, the climber was gone. His dot was replaced by a faint trail going in a straight line over the top of the serac. If the Koreans lost their fourth team member in the fall, then the dot on the photo must be Pakistani Karim, who possibly descended and fell over the serac, setting off the 'waterfall of ice' Marco had noted. Karim wore yellow climbing boots.

Moments later, after receiving the news of Ger's demise, Pemba heard what sounded like a loud explosion and felt as if the whole mountain was falling down around him. He quickly grabbed Marco by the neck and pulled him to safety. An avalanche of rock and ice flowed past them, and in that flow were four bodies, two Koreans and two sherpas. Jumik Bhote, Pasang Bhote and the two Koreans had been hit by a second avalanche. Jumik Bhote had called his pregnant wife by satellite phone from the summit, but never knew that she subsequently gave birth to a baby boy, Jen Jen Mingma. Tsering Bhote luckily was able to shelter from the avalanche under some rocks and was saved. He was devastated – his brother and cousin were dead. Pemba, Marco and Tsering eventually made it back to Camp 4.

Not only was Ger now assumed to be dead but the three climbers he had successfully rescued had been taken by the mountain in this second avalanche. The savage mountain had earned its name, taking eleven climbers that day.

Meanwhile, lost on the mountain, Wilco was suffering badly. He was getting dangerously cold and, about to spend a second night on the mountain, was having a major problem with his feet. He had managed to recharge his sat phone through body heat and, even with snow blindness setting in, was able to dial his phone at home in Utrecht. Heleen, his wife, answered, and Wilco explained the situation. Neither party knew exactly how to end the call. With the help of the Norit webmaster Maarteen van Eck, ExplorersWeb and Thuraya (a mobile satellite communications company), they were able to track Wilco's location through his sat phone by GPS. He was off to the west, somewhere between Camp 3 and Camp 4.

Pemba and Cas, in spite of their exhastion, went back out to find Wilco but failed on the initial attempt. Wilco had to bivvy for a second night on K2. At this point he had had no water or food for some fifty hours; he was exhausted and badly frostbitten. Early on the Sunday morning, Pemba and Cas gave one more search for Wilco. Incredibly, they found him, roughly 150m/500ft from Camp 3, and brought him to safety. The previous night Wilco had bivvied less then 100m/300ft from them and they had not realised it.

Wilco, Pemba and Cas eventually returned to Base Camp. Wilco and Cas were airlifted to Skardu due to their serious frostbite. Miraculously, Pemba – after reaching the summit of K2 on Friday evening and spending a further night on the mountain searching for his friends – was unharmed although he was exhausted. It was a further day before Marco Confortola climbed down to the safety of Base Camp, from where he too was airlifted to hospital.

13. FAMILY TRAVELS TO ISLAMABAD

After receiving the news of Ger's death, the family in Kilcornan was conscious that there were many questions left unanswered. At this time, according to the blogs of other climbers on the mountain, it was believed that Ger had gone up the mountain in the wrong direction because he was disoriented by spending too long at altitude. Another rumour suggested that he refused to come down, and another said that he fell with his good friend Rolf Bae. Yet another rumour suggested that he might have wandered into Chinese territory while lost, and could still be alive. No one had yet received the explanation from Pemba, so rumours abounded and multiplied.

It was decided, in the hope of getting some firm answers, that we would travel to Pakistan to meet the climbers, ask them our questions and collect Ger's gear. Before we left, a friend of the family, John Coleman, came to the house and insisted we take his camcorder with us. 'It's a lot easier to show the family members at home exactly what happened rather than try and explain to them,' he said.

This would be the most important thing we brought to Pakistan. The interviews we recorded would be scrutinised over and over again over the next twelve months and helped to answer a lot of questions. The most important interview we did was with the entire Norit team as they came off the mountain.

Annie Starkey joined J. J., his girlfriend Céren, Denise and me on the trip to Pakistan. We needed to uncover the truth, and establish exactly what had happened on K2.

Ger's sister Denise remembers those fateful days after first hearing the terrible news.

The days that followed were strange – days ran into nights, no concept of time whatsoever – but all I knew was that I really didn't want to go to bed, as my dreams were haunted, haunted by the conviction that it could not be real, that this sort of thing only happens in movies. It's hard to believe something so horrific has happened when you're not there to witness it, and have no remains to prove what we were told was true, that our beloved Ger, my idol, the person I always looked up to throughout my life for having the courage to follow his dreams, was really gone, that he was now lying somewhere on the side of a mountain alone. I couldn't stop wondering what he must have thought in his last moments – did he hear or see the serac fall, or did the giant wave of snow and ice take him unawares and surround him like the bright light we often hear about when you are taken from this earth? I pray he didn't lie there conscious but unable to move, I pray he was taken quickly without suffering. No matter how I tried to convince myself that Ger went quickly, images of him would flash as if I was really there but couldn't help him. I could see him lying there with snow landing on his beard and eyelashes, waking up crying from my sleep. Little did I know those dreams would haunt me for years to come.

The days that followed the accident were filled with mixed emotions – sadness, confusion, but mainly disbelief – as our questions could not be answered. What we thought should have been an easy question produced numerous replies filled with inaccuracies. The one that saddened and confused us the most was the suggestion that Ger had refused to come down. Our reaction was one of disbelief that Ger would not want to come home and see his family again. What could they possibly mean by 'refused to come down'? There was nothing for it but to go to Pakistan, talk to the rest of the expedition and get some clear answers.

Once it was decided that we would go to Pakistan, we knew we had to move quickly, as Denise recalls.

For the trip to Pakistan Pat Falvey sorted out the flights and the Irish embassy did everything in their power to get the paperwork pushed through, rushing visas, etc. Then the thought came into my head: should I go or not? Mum needed us all at home with her but J. J. could do with another family member: why should these things

Team liaison officer Major Kiani in his sitting room with a portrait of Ger on the table.

always fall on his shoulders? So once Damien spoke with his mum and dad to see if they could take care of our two girls, Rebecca and Emma, I thought Mum would be okay as she had my older sisters, Martha and Stephanie, with her. I had a mental battle for a few hours – as that's all the time I had to decide – thinking of how I would react if I saw the mountain while flying in, how would I cope with the pain of knowing Ger was out there, but in the end I decided that Damien and I would go together to Pakistan. But a few phone calls later it turned out the flight was booked out. So unless there was a cancellation, it was not meant to be. But I thought to myself if Ger really wants me there he will make it happen, what will be will be, and the thought had barely crossed my mind when a phone call came to say there was a cancellation in first class. I smiled and said to myself, 'You couldn't make it easy on us, Ger, could ya?'

Our two cousins Mike O'Donoghue and John Nash offered without hesitation to take us to Dublin Airport. In Dublin we would first get a bite to eat at Uncle Seamus and Auntie Ann's, the house that Ger had stayed in at the start of his college years. It was as if I had already started to trace Ger's footsteps, and end up at his final destination. We said tearful goodbyes, and as we answered questions at the airport about why we were going to Pakistan, my eyes welled up again. The flight crew couldn't have been nicer, compassion showing on their faces. At Heathrow the crew on the next leg of our journey had been informed about who we were and so they moved us both up to first class. While we waited for our flight we were brought to a private lounge, for which we were grateful as it was quieter there, which allowed us to gather our thoughts for the journey ahead.

As we alighted from the plane in Pakistan and were hit for the first time by the extreme humidity, thoughts of Ger rushed through my head. The airport may have been basic but our welcome wasn't. Outside arrivals were three men from the Ministry of Tourism, along with Ashgar of Jasmine Tours, which was the Norit expedition tour operator, and Alan Cummins, the Irish ambassador to Iran, as Pakistan doesn't have an Irish embassy. We couldn't believe how much these people had put themselves out for us; they were so kind.

Once outside the airport I felt suffocated as there was not a puff of air. The humidity was off the scale, and the idea of Ger arriving here just amazed me, considering his asthma. He really did suffer badly from it, but I knew the cold mountains suited him.

When we reached our transportation we met Shane Brady, a young man who was working for Concern in Pakistan and who was made aware of our decision to go to Pakistan by his mum who told him that she saw it in the paper and asked if he could do anything for us. Once I learnt of this I really was overcome, to think that a mother and son we had never met could reach out to us in our time of need. I really don't know what we would have done without Shane; I think we would have been lost and confused as to where to go and what to do next. He provided everything we needed, so for this I thank both Mrs Brady and Shane and, of course, Concern for their act of kindness; it will truly never be forgotten.

On our first evening I remember a cloud of apprehension hanging over us as we waited for Wilco and Cas who were airlifted off the mountain due to frostbite. It seemed like an eternity sitting in the house until, finally, we heard the bus pull into the driveway. Annie was first out to meet them, and greeted Wilco and Cas with a big hug, as we all did. Both men later said they were expecting some sort of blame but were relieved to find that we had only come to try and figure it all out. Both men were in a terrible condition and very gaunt looking. The meeting with Wilco and Cas lasted an hour and it was hard for them both as they hadn't met up with the rest of the Norit expedition, and were still trying to piece together what had happened.

Two days later we met with the entire Norit team and it was sad to have pictures taken with them and accept that Ger was not coming home.

The following interview was recorded with members of the Norit expedition in a house owned by the Irish aid agency Concern. The temperature was almost unbearable and the noise of the air conditioning unit was deafening. Those present at the meeting were J. J., Denise, Annie, Céren, myself, Wilco, Cas and Pemba (the latter three had been on the summit that day) and the other three members of the Norit K2 Dutch International Expedition, Jelle Staleman, Mark Sheen and Roeland van Oss, who had been on K2 at Base Camp, but for one reason or another had not made a summit bid on 1 August. All gathered around the small coffee table. Annie was the first to speak.

> **Annie:** Ger's mom, she had a strong feeling – a clear feeling – that Ger wanted us to come out here and give you all a hug.
>
> **Mark:** Ah yeah, this is Ger's passport and wallet as it was, I don't know who to give it to. (Mark looks around nervously and Annie gets up and takes the items.)
>
> **Annie:** Thanks, Mark. You know Ger always talked about a great night in a tent at Broad Peak with you.
>
> **Mark** (smiling): Ah, that would be Camp 1, we kept rolling on top of each other and we were talking about what we would do to the tent. We were going to throw it off the cliffs behind us when we were finished with it.
>
> Annie laughs as she listens.
>
> **Mark:** I remember that night fondly, the thing about Ger was we laughed. The night was nice but the tent was too small, but even though it was uncomfortable, Ger's sense of humour is what I loved about the guy. I'm born the same date as Ger, only Ger was born five years earlier, he's the only person I'd ever met that shared the same birth date as me.
>
> **Annie** (laughs): Oh really? That's funny.

Mark: Yeah, it is.

Annie: And Pemba, of course, he [Ger] really talked highly about you, you're a really good friend.

Pemba (shyly): Yeah okay, I just can't believe it.

Denise: My mother has heard all about you, Pemba.

Annie: Now, you found Marco, right?

Pemba: Yeah, yeah, below the couloir [base of the Bottleneck].

Annie: Did you see Ger?

Pemba: Ahh … ah no, I didn't, all casualties just in front of me, two Koreans and two sherpas only metres from me and Marco. Same time I am taking care of Marco, multi-serac fell down. Sherpas and Koreans were rolling down the couloir, then when the avalanche stopped I could see two bodies, the other two were at the other side but the visibility was too poor.

Annie: Okay, but Marco saw Ger?

Pemba: Pardon? (Pemba looks puzzled at the question.)

Annie: Marco saw Ger?

Pemba: Marco at the time was exactly 8,000m/26,000ft elevation, he is also flat lying down on the snow. The other sherpas were couple hundred [metres] ahead of me so same time they rolling down – me and Marco are okay metres from the chute but safe.

Jelle: I spoke with Marco at Base Camp. He told me he saw the two La Sportiva boots, the kind Ger was wearing, so it was probably him in the snow. I don't remember exactly what he said.

Cas: Did you see something, Pemba? Did you see persons falling down?

Pemba: Ah no. Only sherpa [Pasang Bhote] before he fall down by serac talk to me on walkie talkie: 'Ah okay Pemba, there is one member fall down on Traverse because hit by serac.' Then visibility was very poor and you cannot see 3 or 4m [10 or 13ft] in front of you.

Cas: Yeah, I understand. Sometimes it was clear and other times it was covered with clouds.

Pemba: I then ask the sherpa, 'Can you identify him?' And he told me red and black down suit, red and black down suit. I'll say definitely Gerard.

Cas: I am asking you that because we were talking in this same room two days ago. We were trying to explain the whole story with what Wilco knew and what I knew with drawings and things.

Pemba: There are three people I didn't see – Gerard, Mr Hugues and Karim, those three people no sign of on second day.

Cas: I saw Hugues.

Pemba: Because of poor visibility I count eight dots on mountain. Eight dots, they are all here but during the afternoon when I am with Marco on couloir, I look up and try to see everyone but not possible. I saw two Koreans and two sherpas and I am still unable to see Gerard, Hugues or Karim. When the sherpa talk to me on the radio he tell me Ger's suit red and black. This to me is Gerard, because the Koreans [do] not [have] a complete red down suit, Hugues doesn't have a red suit and Karim has a pure red suit.

Cas: Already we were talking but Hugues fell down next to me, he fell very close to me. So why I am asking you is that you were lower than the body of Gerard so you have not seen him. The family would like to have as much evidence as possible. This is another fact, that the sherpa has seen his suit, this we didn't know, we only heard the story of Marco and the two boots or something. They want to have as much assurance that it was Gerard and that he's not walking across China.

Jelle: Pemba, Roeland and an American guy tried to make a report at Base Camp; they tried to talk to a lot of people and piece together what happened. When we get that report, it might be clearer what happened; we hope it will solve a lot of questions. At first we thought Ger just fell down but later we find out hit by serac, that's the reason he fell.

Pemba: Main cause hit by serac.

Cas: This is different here. Marco says that they were next to three Koreans hanging on ropes, then he says Gerard was going up and of course the only one there to see anything was Marco. We have been trying to figure out why Gerard would have gone up, but now we listen to your stories we know Marco has been telling more stories.

Pemba: I could not get any more information from this sherpa [Pasang Bhote] as five minutes later he too was dead.

So the key to evidence of Ger's death, visual evidence based on his climbing suit, was received on radio phone by Pemba from the sherpa Pasang Bhote who was killed almost immediately after.

The exchange above also gives some indication of the communication difficulties among the many different nationalities climbing on K2 that season, which, as Ger had noted in his log, included Korean, Serbian, Dutch, Nepalese, Italian, Basque, French, Norwegian, Swedish and American, all apparently attempting to use English as a *lingua franca*.

Marco had stated that he had secured the climbers and left after calling for help. According to an investigation after the event carried out by ExplorersWeb, no call was ever received. As the interview continued Pemba reported that Marco had spoken of three Koreans left for dead; there were, in fact, only two Koreans and Jumik Bhote. These were the three people who were coming slowly down the mountain when they met up with Tsering and Pasang Bhote. Pemba claims that the Bhotes had not climbed up willingly, but had been forced by the leader of the Korean expedition to go back up the mountain and search for the three missing Korean expedition members, in spite of bad weather, the unstable serac overhanging the route and debris fallen on the route itself. Pemba says he went up himself, hoping to find Ger, but found Marco, and could climb no further as conditions were too dangerous. Sure enough, shortly after finding Marco, Pemba witnessed another serac fall which killed the two Koreans, who had been slowly coming down the mountain, and two sherpas, Jumik Bhote and his cousin Pasang.

Pemba is unable to confirm the fate of the French climber Hugues, or that of his climbing partner, Karim. He describes the climb down from the summit in the dark, before the climbers got separated:

> **Cas:** When did you see Hugues for the last time? When did you pass him? I was passing him just before the Traverse.
>
> **Pemba:** Hugues, Gerard, Wilco and Karim were all together with one fixed rope, then Marco and two sherpas, Tsering and Jumik, are at the back. Me and 'Little' Pasang [Pasang Bhote] from Korean team, we are in front because when we descend together we are about 8,400m/27,600ft. When finally it's getting dark, we are four sherpas. We decide two go in front and two stay behind because we need to check true trail and anchor measurement and anchor point on the top of the Bottleneck. We have to find the anchor point [so that we can abseil down], for that we need a good detection. Jumik and Tsering stay behind ... They are a good distance between us – so when we had reached the anchor then we communicate with Jumik Sherpa and tell him, 'Okay now, this is anchor point so we need everyone to descend here.'

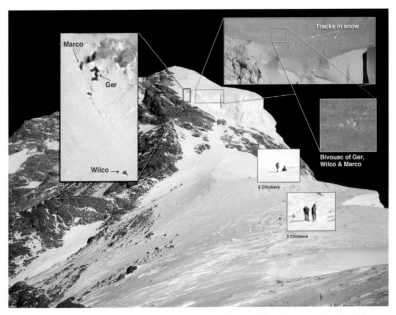

This photo by Lars Nessa shows the situation on the upper slopes of K2 at 8 a.m. on Saturday 2 August 2008.

This photo by Pemba Gyalje was taken at 9.59 a.m. on Saturday 2 August 2008.

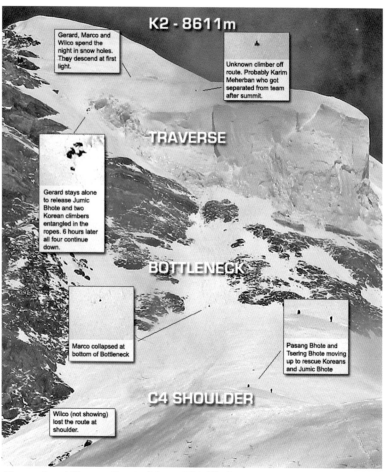

K2 upper slope at 10 a.m. on Saturday 2 August 2008. This photo was taken by Pemba Gyalje from Camp 4 before he went back up the mountain to assist Marco Confortola. (Courtesy ExplorersWeb)

> When we reach the couloir there is nothing, no fixed line, no anchor.

Pemba repeated a lot of his facts again to the team, but the most important thing that we discovered from the meeting was that Ger went back up, and that Marco descended, presuming all were dead. Pemba found the explanation that Ger had gone up to give a fixed line more slack totally plausible: 'Because we know about Gerard's good manners. He always wanted to help.' Nearly six hours later the Koreans and Jumik Sherpa were descending slowly and met

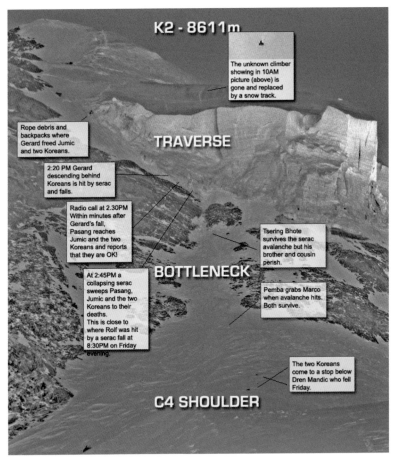

K2 upper slope at 7 p.m. on Saturday 2 August 2008. Pemba Gyalje took this photo from Camp 4 after returning to the camp with Marco Confortola. (Courtesy ExplorersWeb)

with 'Big' Pasang [Pasang Bhote], who witnessed Ger coming behind them, before a serac fell and hit him. From Pemba's testimony and the timeline on the mountain we could see that Ger had not died until after the three stranded climbers had been freed. They were descending slowly, followed by Ger who had successfully rescued them, when disaster struck, killing first Ger, and then the climbers along with an additional sherpa who had gone up to help in the rescue.

At the end of the meeting some pictures were taken of the team with the family. J. J. and Denise presented the expedition with an Irish flag with a picture of Ger in the centre, and J. J. invited them to Ireland to attend a Mass that was arranged for the following Sunday to celebrate Ger's wonderful life.

Photo taken by Pemba Gyalje at 7.16 p.m. on Saturday 2 August 2008.

14. MEDIA VERSUS THE McDONNELLS: HOME FROM PAKISTAN

Coming away from that meeting in Pakistan a clearer picture was beginning to develop of events on K2. The family was slowly piecing together what had happened and how Ger had gone back up the mountain to rescue the three stranded climbers. Unfortunately, the initial stories that had reached the family had also reached the media. It is not completely surprising, given that several of the accounts of climbers on the mountain seemed to suggest a different story unless they were examined together. The confusion and absolute disaster of that day's events meant that the stories were equally confused. Climbers could only recount what they thought to be the facts as they remembered them. Stories changed as new facts were presented, and sometimes changed again to try to reconcile the conflicting stories. Climbers who were exhausted and near the point of collapse and doing their best to survive could only recall events as they appeared to them at the time.

Marco, who had spent several hours with Ger trying to free the Korean climbers, gave several interviews in which he said he thought both the Koreans and Ger had perished before he was rescued by Pemba. All the evidence tells us this is not the case, but there is no doubt he believed he had seen his friend Ger perish. Ger was swept away by a falling serac but Pemba's video interview – describing the descending climbers being followed by a figure that could only have been Ger – suggests that Marco was mistaken and that he had seen the remains of Hugues' Pakistani climbing companion Karim.

A story that surfaced on 12 November entitled 'Heroes in Fine Print' by Freddie Wilkinson (*Huffington Post*, 12 November 2008) summed up the

171

media reporting. While the key and laudable element of the story was the heroism of the sherpas on K2, how it – and the media generally – reported on Ger was very tough on the family.

> 'On the mountain there were no heroes,' K2 survivor Cas van de Gevel was recently quoted as saying in *Outside* magazine, 'just an unspoken agreement that you help as much as you can.'
>
> *Outside* and *Men's Journal* recently published feature-length pieces on the K2 disaster. Both stories lead with the tale of three European men, Wilco van Rooijen, Gerard McDonnell and Marco Confortola, who bivouacked at nearly 28,000 feet [8,500m] after the catastrophic serac avalanche stripped the Bottleneck Couloir of its fixed ropes on the evening of 1 August. The next day, they were forced to climb down the Bottleneck un-roped. Along the way they passed a party of distressed Korean climbers; the three abandoned them to continue their own descents to safety. Two of them made it, but McDonnell was swept to his death in an avalanche.
>
> While Confortola and van Rooijen can hardly be faulted for not doing more, it does seem like their teammate Cas van de Gevel is right – the tragedy was a grim game of Russian roulette. It was every man for himself.

While no one could have faulted Ger and his fellow climbers had they descended to save their own lives in such terrible circumstances, this story and many others like it did not reflect the truth as the family knew it. When the story began to emerge from the remaining climbers that Ger had done something extraordinary on K2 it seemed hard to believe. Wilco told the press that anyone going back up the mountain at that stage would have been near suicidal. Marco could not believe that Ger would knowingly decide to go back up the mountain to attempt a rescue after having already spent hours trying to free the entangled climbers. At first, Marco shouting to Ger to come back as he climbed back up the mountain was portrayed in the media as a sad footnote to the disaster on K2 – a sad portrayal of an experienced climber overcome by the mountain and the elements.

The days and weeks passed and everything seemed surreal to the family. Ger was gone and many questions remained unanswered, and the papers gave their own opinions as to what happened.

Facing page: On 4 August 2009, one year and two days after the awful events on K2, David Watson skied down the Bottleneck. David climbed Everest twice and is the only person to have skied down the infamous Bottleneck on K2.

Annie had been keeping an eye on all the reports and was replying to all the blogs. Freddie Wilkinson's 'Heroes in Fine Print' story caught her attention as it went on after the above quote to accuse the western world of not recognising the sherpas' bravery, in particular Chhiring Dorje's decision to abseil down the Bottleneck with his fellow sherpa Pasang Lama [Pasang Bhote], who lacked an ice axe, strapped to his body. Annie emailed Freddie and gave him the raw facts as they were, outlining how Ger died trying to save the lives of others. Freddie was shocked at this and was intrigued to find out more. He wrote another article exactly one month later titled 'The Abandonment of Gerard McDonnell'. Slowly the story was beginning to get out. Freddie Wilkinson's piece, revisiting his earlier article on the heroic actions of the sherpas on K2, acknowledged that there were also other heroes on the mountain.

> I learned months ago in email correspondence with Pemba that the rescue team had succeeded in reaching Jumik Bhote and two of the Koreans. But it wasn't until I met with him in Kathmandu and we had the chance to speak extensively about K2 that I heard about the man in the red suit behind Jumik and the Koreans. Though both Gerard McDonnell and Pakistani guide Karim Meherban wore red suits, only McDonnell's had patches on the front matching the description given in the radio transmission. Accordingly, Pemba believes that this man was his friend and teammate McDonnell.
>
> The precise circumstances of Gerard McDonnell's disappearance has been one of the most enduring questions of the K2 tragedy. A story written by Omar Waraich in the UK paper *The Independent* on August 9th (purportedly based on Mr Confortola's first newspaper interview after the tragedy) seemed to suggest that the three Koreans [*sic*] died in their presence: 'For three hours, McDonnell and Confortola tried to right them, but it was in vain. All three died. It was at that moment, 'for some strange reason', that McDonnell began to walk away.'
>
> A lengthy article in *Men's Journal* written by Matt Powers (who also was in Islamabad interviewing the survivors) reported that: 'By mid-morning, Marco and Gerard had left the Koreans and continued towards the Traverse … Suddenly, Marco said later, Gerard turned around and began to climb back up the slope, back towards the Koreans, offering no explanation.' Finally, Michael

Kodas wrote in *Outside* magazine that: 'They spent three and a half hours trying to free the Koreans but gave up when the glacier let loose nearby and reminded them of their perilous location. McDonnell, perhaps confused by the lack of oxygen, climbed back up the slope towards the summit. Confortola shouted to his friend but couldn't get his attention. Then he heard an avalanche and recognized two yellow boots in the slide.'

Pemba's account of the radio transmission requires that the overall tragedy be re-examined. It seems possible, if not probable, that Gerard McDonnell continued efforts to revive Jumik Bhote and the two Koreans after van Rooijen and Confortola descended, and that McDonnell succeeded in getting the injured climbers mobile so that they could descend the Traverse to the top of the Bottleneck, where they were met by the rescue team of Pasang Bhote and Tsering Bhote. Sadly, many published accounts have portrayed McDonnell's final actions as being irrational, perhaps the result of hypoxia or hallucination. It now seems quite likely that McDonnell nobly continued rescue efforts right up until the moment he was killed.

After his investigations Wilkinson said:

It is readily clear that the media owes the family, friends and loved ones of Gerard McDonnell an apology for so misrepresenting his memory. As someone who's written about K2 a lot, I include myself as being partly to blame. In 'Heroes in Fine Print' I implied that McDonnell, along with van Rooijen and Confortola, had abandoned the Koreans, while the sherpas launched a rescue. Abandoned is a very strong word, and it bears nothing in common with what I now believe were Gerard McDonnell's final actions.

Others were also interested in the story and ExplorersWeb pieced the story together using the testimony of the surviving climbers, photos taken on K2 and the known timelines of radio calls on the mountain. Their conclusion was without doubt.

This, for us and for Annie, was groundbreaking. Were Ger's final acts of heroism finally going to be known to the world? Many tried to deny it but one night when J. J., Denise and I were scanning over the different photos from Ger's camera they came across the two photos that showed, when viewed in close-up, the rescue efforts carried out by Ger and the shadow of a climber way off course on the mountain sitting in a bivouac. A similar picture taken that evening shows that both the climbers and the lone person in the bivouac were gone, with a snow trail going over the edge of the mountain from where the lone climber was (see pages 167–170).

Over the next few weeks the family worked with Tom and Tina Sjogren, founders of the prestigious ExplorersWeb, and the pieces started to fit together. From Pemba's story everyone knew about the first radio call regarding Marco but not so many knew about the second call about Ger being spotted behind the rescued climbers.

In January 2009 ExplorersWeb had Ger at number one in their 'Best of 2008 Awards for Heroism and Bravery':

> The most selfless effort was made by Irish Gerard McDonnell, who after two nights on K2's upper slopes including one in an open bivouac, resolved to alone stay and help two Korean climbers and a Nepali sherpa, climbers he didn't know. Gerard knew well that his effort seriously put his own life at risk. His action is almost unmatched on the 8,000ers. Gerard's incredible courage and compassion were rendered fruitless when the survivors were killed in a final avalanche. Tragically, their rescuer lost his life as well. This probably would not have been the case had Gerard simply followed his mates Marco and Wilco down, both alive today. Without the final serac falls, Gerard's, the Bhotes' and the Koreans' story would have had a different ending. Yet their deaths can't change the spirit displayed. Gerard was called 'Jesus' by his peers. 'Hero' is a better word.

At last the true story was getting out. But had the family members not gone to Pakistan following the tragedy, this might never have been the case.

15. IMMEDIATE AFTERMATH AND LEGACY

What Ger McDonnell did that fateful day on K2 was no surprise to those who knew him. 'Gerard was not only True Mountain and an adventure-loving person but also a pure and unselfish climber,' said Pemba Gyalje. After spending three hours with Marco Confortola trying to free the Koreans and Jumik, Ger spent up to another six hours alone until he finally freed all three tangled climbers.

Thanks to Pemba's photographic evidence, the people who investigated this tragedy were able to put together the final hours of Ger's life. He was never going to leave anyone in trouble. Ger would never have been able to live with himself if he did not at least try and help those people.

Some of the stories you have read in this book demonstrate that character in Ger. He was competitive, ambitious and totally committed. And with Ger it was a case of 'what you see is what you get'. He never hesitated to help out or contribute to any climb he was on. He was a climber's climber. Alan Arnette, the American climber, once said, 'If you had the misfortune of being stuck in a tent for days waiting out a storm, your fortune would be to spend it with Ger.'

The memorial Mass for Ger was set for 17 August 2008. The whole parish of Kilcornan and the surrounding parishes did everything in their power to make this a very special day for the family. It was called the 'Celebration of the Life of Ger McDonnell'. Ger's life started on the night of a huge storm and on the day of the memorial the weather was equally wet and windy.

A huge marquee was set up in the community grounds and the adjoining hall was also set up for the crowds that were expected to arrive. The Taoiseach and then President McAleese were both represented. Members of Ger's Norit team were present as was the director of Norit Ireland, Ivan Rigney. A large contingent from the Irish climbing community arrived on the day to say goodbye to their friend. It was a beautiful ceremony and concluded with the family releasing white doves into the sky in memory of Ger. And although the rain poured down that day, thousands turned out to offer their condolences.

The McDonnells, Kilcornan and Ireland had lost a special son and now it was time to put him to rest. Kíla, Ger's favourite band, played at the funeral Mass and also performed on the stage afterwards for friends and family who wanted to remember Ger in happy ways. Gertie and the family could scarcely believe the support that was shown by people from all over, especially their own parish of Kilcornan. We will be forever grateful to them. The night ended late and people laughed and cried as stories were shared about Ger.

Weeks later, the family went to Alaska to celebrate the life of Ger again with his friends there. It was another beautiful occasion; Annie had organised a tree-planting ceremony in the local park where there were hundreds of trees planted in Ger's memory.

Later that year the McDonnell family, in conjunction with the Mountain Fund Organisation, set up the Gerard McDonnell Memorial Fund, whose summary ran as follows:

> Gerard McDonnell had a big heart. His compassion and strength of character was apparent in everything he did.

Joelle Brupbacher met with the Bhote children while presenting money on behalf of the McDonnell family to the Gerard McDonnell Memorial Fund. (Courtesy Amanda Padoan)

First recipient of the DCU scholarship award, Tadhg Reynolds, (centre) with Ger's sisters Martha (left) and Denise (right).

On August 1, 2008 Gerard summited K2 and made mountaineering history as the first Irish person to stand on the summit. The next morning, he risked his life to rescue three climbers stranded above 8,000 metres [26,000ft]. Upon descent, Gerard and the men he saved were lost in an avalanche. Those who knew Gerard understand he could never walk away from anyone who needed help.

To honour his spirit, the Gerard McDonnell Memorial Fund was established to assist the children of those Pakistani and Nepalese climbers who also lost their lives on K2 in 2008: Jehan Baig, Karim Meherban, Jumik Bhote and Pasang Bhote.

The Fund will sponsor these children throughout their childhood years, helping with their education and medical care. The

Mountain Fund staff is 100% volunteer, and there are no deductions for overheads. Your donation goes directly to the children.

In October 2008 Coillte asked the McDonnells to plant a tree beside the original one in Curraghchase which Ger himself had planted, in recognition of his great achievements. In his book, *K2: Life and Death on the World's Most Dangerous Mountain*, Ed Viesturs tells of how the story of the dramatic events on K2 in August 2008 caught the imagination of adventurers worldwide, and was discussed with a passion on websites and in blogs. The heroic part in the tragedy played by the sherpas was especially praised, and there was international rejoicing when Pemba Gyalje, Ger's climbing partner on both Everest and K2, was named as Adventurer of the Year by *National Geographic Adventure* in December 2008. The National Geographic Society flew Pemba to Washington DC for the ceremony, where he received a standing ovation. In February 2009 the American Alpine Club gave its most presitigous honour, awarded for saving the lives of other climbers, to Pemba at its annual meeting in Golden, Colorado.

After Ger's funeral, a close group of neighbours and friends purchased a young oak tree for the family. The gesture was beautiful as the tree represents longevity and strength and its life-affirming symbolism is significant to a family that lost a loved one but did not have the body returned to them.

In 2009 Dublin City University, the college Ger attended, introduced a scholarship fund named after him.

> As a testament to Ger's warmth of character, family, friends, classmates and the DCU School of Engineering came together to establish a permanently endowed scholarship fund in his memory. The Ger McDonnell Memorial Access Scholarship Fund is being run as part of the University's Access Programme. Now in its 20th year, the DCU Access Scholarship Programme provides over 400 talented students with the opportunity of a third level education, which their circumstances would not otherwise allow.

On 30 April 2010 the scholarship was officially launched. A plaque was unveiled by the chairman of DCU's Educational Trust, Larry Quinn.

> We are delighted to report that over €56,000 has been raised for the Ger McDonnell Memorial Access Scholarship Fund with the first scholarship being awarded to a student studying Engineering

at DCU. Because the scholarship is endowed, a scholarship will be awarded in Ger's name to a deserving DCU student each year in perpetuity.

A former classmate of Ger's in DCU, Fiona McDonnell, spoke of the importance of the scholarship.

> One of the reasons Ger was so well known and respected by so many people was because of his commitment to helping others. It's fitting that he be remembered within DCU by an Access Scholarship that can help someone else. Although the scholarship can in no way compensate for the loss of Ger, it is our hope that, in time, it will bring some small measure of comfort to all who knew Ger in the knowledge that his memory is encouraging the potential of bright young students at DCU. Dublin City University is deeply honoured to house this special tribute to Ger and we look forward to sharing news of the scholarship recipients in the years to come.

In 2009 Limerick County Council named a sports award after Ger to recognise 'unsung heroes in local fields of sport'. Commenting on Ger's association with the award, Phelim Macken, Limerick Sports Partnership Coordinator, stated, 'Gerard was a proud Limerick man who pushed the boundaries of human endurance to the limits. His appetite for life was an inspiration to anyone who came into contact with him. I wish to sincerely thank Gerard's family and friends for approving his association with the award. I also wish to thank the many people from across Limerick who nominated representatives from their local clubs and organisations.'

Also in 2009 Ger's family presented the Irish Club of Alaska with the Gerard McDonnell Memorial Award, which the club presents annually to the person nominated as having 'best contributed to the Irish Music/Dance/Culture and community of Alaska'.

> The Irish Club of Alaska's Holiday Ceili on November 14th at the Snow Goose Theater was a great success, both financially for the Gerard McDonnell Memorial Scholarship Fund and the recipient of this year's award, Willow Feighery.
> Gerard McDonnell (1971–2008) was a beloved member of the Alaska Irish Music Community. Gerard's musical abilities were well respected in the community. He encouraged young people

Members of the McDonnell family receive the Pinzolo International Alpine Solidarity gold medal on Ger's behalf. The medal was awarded to Ger in recognition of his bravery on K2. Back row (*l–r*): Paul Whiting, Irish Mountain Rescue Association, and John Dowd, Kerry Mountain Rescue Team. Front row (*l–r*): J. J., Denise, Gertie, Martha and Stephanie.

to participate in Irish music, dance and promoting those arts in Alaska. Gerard was born in Ireland but considered Alaska his home away from home.

In September 2010 the McDonnell family were invited to travel to Italy to receive, on Ger's behalf, the Gold Medal Award as part of the International Italian Silver Plaque Award given to climbers who are recognised for their bravery on the mountains. Ireland Mountain Rescue's nomination of Ger was unanimously accepted.

The Pinzolo International Alpine Solidarity Award was born back in 1972, and ever since, year after year, it awards those who have distinguished themselves in alpine rescue operations. The Silver Plaque gets its inspiration from the simplicity and straightforwardness of mountain people and from the principles of true human solidarity; it awards those who leave home, work and family apart, to run there where someone needs help, without asking anything in exchange.

Ger received the Gold Medal this year after the Committee unanimously decided to accept Ireland Mountain Rescue's proposal and award the Gold Medal to 'Ger' McDonnell. The award consists of a Silver Plaque and a Golden Medal with the engraved reason for the award. This acknowledgement is a symbol for the human and moral values of those who sacrifice themselves to other people. From its 25th edition on, the prize has been supported by the High Patronage of the President of the Italian Republic and the particular blessing of the Pope.

In 2009 Jelle Staleman, the Dutch climber who was with Ger as part of the Norit expedition in 2008, was climbing with his friend Niek de Jonge in Greenland on some unclimbed and unnamed peaks. On 25 August they climbed what subsequently became known as McDonnell Peak. Jelle recalls the decision to name the mountain.

We were making preparations in Holland already and we looked at the maps and saw that 90 per cent of the mountains in this area in Greenland didn't have a name. That's really why we ended up

McDonnell Peak in Greenland. (Courtesy Jelle Staleman)

Jeff Jessen and Connie Rogg erecting the plaque to Ger on King Mountain in Alaska, 2008.

In Memory of Our Beloved Friend:

Gerard "Ger" McDonnell

Born: January 20, 1971, Kilcornan, County Limerick, Ireland
Died: August 2, 2008, Karakoram, Pakistan

"Sin e anois a cháirde. Ta an t-am ag teacht."

The first Irishman to reach the summit of K2, Ger died heroically
on the descent while helping injured climbers.

*"Greater love hath no man than this, that a man lay down his life
for his friends."*
John 15:13

there. We started thinking about what kind of name we'd call our mountain. My wish all the time was to name it something like McDonnell Peak but my climbing partner never met Ger and I guess it was a bit unfair on him. But he had followed the Norit K2 expedition so he knew all that Ger did and what had happened to him. When in early January 2009 Ger received the ExplorersWeb award we both agreed that it would be nice to name the mountain after him. A tribute for the person he was.

On 17 August 2008, the same weekend as Ger's memorial service in Kilcornan, a group of Ger's friends in Alaska – Amber McDonough, her husband Jim, Jeff Jessen, Connie Rogg and Butch Allen – erected a memorial to him on King Mountain. Amber recalls the nine-hour adventure.

We started early and blew up packrafts upriver of King Mountain. We crossed the Matanuska River, stashed our gear in trees (to keep the bears and critters from tearing it up), and then started bushwhacking toward the mountain. Eventually we found some rough game trails and gained in elevation. When we started, the mountain was totally obscured by clouds so we didn't even know if we could make it to the top.

It was a tough, steep climb through birch and spruce forests and devil club (very nasty). Eventually we crested a ridge and could see a beautiful lake below us. Then we realised that we had to descend again before we could tackle the main mountain. The lake had some arctic loons crying out and swimming around on it. Then we resumed climbing, up and up past the vegetation, and took a break for a snack. As we were leaving we noticed blueberry bear scat nearby – hard to believe a bear would roam so high up, but they do.

We kept going into the cloud fog and saw a bird's nest with four very camouflaged eggs and we saw an ermine weasel evade us. Soon we were wondering if we could keep going. We were on a knife ridge and heard rock falling in the mist. We didn't know if it was a bear so we called out. It was eerie, but then the clouds somehow lifted and we saw sheep above us and blue sky! We climbed into huge scree fields and lots of broken rock. It was rough going, but the weather was improving so we were encouraged. We made it close to the top and found the perfect slab of rock upon which to place the plaque. We affixed it to the rock and Jim read the words aloud.

We took photos of the memorial with the Irish flag and Nepali prayer flags and listened to Gerard's voice singing 'Molly Brannigan'. It was so great to hear Gerard's voice. We all cried and were silent. Gerard would have been proud of us.

We hung prayer flags and brought the flag of Ireland up and down the mountain with us because we knew it was important to him. We thought a pointed rock looked like K2. The weather was turning so we said our goodbyes and headed down. One of the best parts happened during our descent when a beautiful rainbow appeared. We all agreed Ger was with us then.

On 1 August 2009, the first anniversary of Ger reaching the summit of K2, over a hundred friends and family members came from all over the country to meet up at Cronin's Yard at the base of Corrán Tuathail in County Kerry to climb what for many would be their own Everest. They did this to commemorate the life of Ger and to celebrate the numerous remarkable achievements throughout his short life.

It was a wonderful day and over the following weeks – organised by Ger's brother-in-law Barry and 'Banjo' Bannon – a plaque was mounted at the cross

In Memory of
Ger McDonnell
(Gearóid MacDomhnaill)
Killeen, Kilcornan,
Co.Limerick
Born 20th of January
1971 Died On 2nd
of August 2008 on K2
The first Irishman to
reach the summit of K2
Who died heroically on
the descent having helped
injured climbers
Ar dheis Dé go raibh a anam
Erected by family,friends
and fellow climbers
Because of his love
of Carrauntuohil

Ger's niece and goddaughter, Rebecca O'Brien, aged six, made the climb to the top of Corrán Tuathail in memory of her uncle in 2009.

at the top of Corrán Tuathail. This was a special place for Ger and now he would be remembered there for ever.

One day, my daughter Rebecca, Ger's niece and goddaughter, was asking questions about how and why her uncle died. For the children it was hard as they were young and Ger would have only been home maybe two or three times a year as they were growing up.

Ger's plaque had been erected on top of Corrán Tuathail and Rebecca, or Becca as she prefers, wanted to see it. I was not keen on the idea and, having only been up there a few times myself, needed the help of close friend Brian O'Keefe to guide us.

The Gilkey Memorial following the 2008 disaster with some of the plaques erected to the eleven climbers who died: Dren Mandić, Jehan Baig, Rolf Bae, Hugues D'Aubarède, Karim Meherban, Gerard McDonnell, Jumik Bhote, Pasang Bhote, Park Kyeong-hyo, Kim Hyo-gyeong and Hwang Dong-jin. (COURTESY WILCO VAN ROOIJEN)

The memorial plate erected at the Gilkey Memorial by the Norit team. (COURTESY ASHGAR ALI PORIK, DIRECTOR OF JASMINE TOURS).

He gladly brought Becca and me up the Zig-zag route and Becca, as proud as a peacock, stood beside the memorial plaque dedicated to her uncle. At six years of age she had climbed Ireland's highest peak in memory of Uncle Ger. When asked would she do it again she replied, 'Why? Sure I've already climbed it!'

Wherever Ger is, you can be sure he is smiling down on us all. He fulfilled his dream of conquering K2, but he achieved so much more by doing so. Ger was unique, and we hope you can understand that from reading his story.

INDEX

Pictures are indicated by page numbers in bold.

Abruzzi, Duke of 44
Abruzzi Glacier 28
Abruzzi route 44–5, 73, 86, **127**
Adare 105, 139–41
Aksai Chin plateau 109
Alaska 17–23, 37–43, 63–9, 108–9, 136,
    138, 141–2, 145, 146, 178, 181–2,
    185–6; *see also* Denali
Allen, Butch 185
American Alpine Club 180
American team 4–5, 6, 78, 86
Anchorage 39, 63–9, 111, 141–2, 146
Antarctica 71, 96, 135–7
Arnette, Alan 177
Askeaton 30, 32, 33
Askole 24–5, **27**, 119

Bae, Rolf 8, **10**, 11–12, 78, 135, 148, 152,
    157, **188**
Baig, Jehan 6, 13, 179, **188**
Baltoro Glacier 26, 28
Bannon, Banjo 128–9, 133, 186
Basque route *see* Cesen route
Ben Nevis 69
Bhote, Jumik 13, 77, 152–4, 156–8, 166,
    168–9, 174–5, 176, 177, 179, **188**
Bhote, Pasang 78, 152, 155–6, 157–8,
    164–6, 175, 176, 179, **188**
Bhote, Tsering 77–8, 152, 155–6, 158, 166,
    175
Bite, Hoselito 125–7

Bold Peak 20
Brady, Shane 162
Braldu River 25
Broad Peak 15, 46, 86, 103, **115**, **117**, 117–23
Brupbacher, Joelle 119, **128**, 129, 133, **178**

Cabot, Red 135–6
Camp Jhula 25
Cardozo, John 37
Cesen, Tomo 44
Cesen route 44–5, 73, 77, 86
China 109–11
Chombi (sherpa) 82
Coleman, John 64, 67, 68, 159
Collins, Con 118
Concordia 28
Confortola, Marco **7**, 7, 11, 13, **15**, 152–8,
    153, 164–6, 168, 171, 173–7
Cork 104
Corrán Tuathail 107, 186–9, **187**
Crean, Tom 135–6
Croke Park 138
Crowley, Aleister 44
Crowley, Cian 79, 94
Crowley, Darragh 79
Crowley, ShaWne 79, **80**, 94–5
Cummins, Alan 162
Curraghchase Forest Park 28, 105, 108, 180

d'Aubarède, Hugues 8, **10**, 12, 45, 78, 125,
    152, 156, 165, 166, **188**

de Jonge, Niek 183
Deadhorse 63, 138
Denali
    climbs 22–3, 48–57, **51**, 111–13, **112**,
        113, 138–9
    training for 17–22, 39, 43
Doolin 34
Dorje, Chhiring 12, 152, 174
Dowd, John 111–13, **113**, 118, 120, 123–4,
    182
Downes, Tom **31**
Drive for Life 79, **80**, **81**, 93–5, 108
Dublin City University (DCU) 33, 34–5,
    180–81

Eckenstein, Oscar 44
England 33
Everest
    2003 expedition 2, 15, 62, 72, 78–85, **80**,
        81, 87–96
    compared to K2 2, 16
    Ger plans to climb 63, 69–71
    Hillary and Norgay's ascent 14
    homecoming from expedition **104**,
        104–8, **106**, **108**
ExplorersWeb 157, 158, 166, 175–6

Fairbanks 142
Falvey, Pat
    aftermath of Ger's death 147, 148, 149,
        160
    Antarctic expedition 136–7
    Denali climb **113**
    Everest expedition (2003) 69–72, 78,
        82–3, 87–9, 91–3, 95–6
    Everest homecoming 104, 105–6, **108**
Freddie T. Bear 72, **81**, **108**
French team 74, 77

Gasherbrum II 46
Gasherbrum mountains 28, 46
Geeting, Doug 52
Gilkey, Art 97
Gilkey Memorial 97, **98**, **188**
Go Mi-sun 12, 152
Godwin Austin Glacier 28, 44
Great Smoky Mountains 37
Greece 33
Greenland 183–5
Griffin, Bridget 105
Gyalje, Pemba

aftermath of Ger's death 163–9, 171,
    174, 176, 177
Everest expedition (2003) 2, 62, 78, 79,
    83–4, 87–9, 91, 96
K2 expedition (2008) 1–2, **5**, 5–12, **9**,
    10, 14, 46–7, **47**, 59, 74–5, 87, 98–9,
    126–7, 152, 155–8
named Adventurer of the Year 180

Hackett, Peter 48
Haegens, Court 74, 75, 99–100
Hall, Laura 40–42
Hancock, Dave 119
Hanley, Tom **31**, 33
Hanly, John 66
Herzenberg, Karen 69
Hillary, Sir Edmund 14, 95, 106–7
Holland, Aisling **41**
Holland, Aoife **41**
Holland, Stephen **41**
Hwang Dong-jin **188**

Independent 174
International Italian Silver Plaque Award
    182–3
Irish Club of Alaska 181–2
Islamabad 14, 24, 118, 159–69
Italian team 86, 103

Jessen, Jeff 18–22, 43, 48, 50–51, 52, 53,
    184, 185
Joyce, John 91

K2
    2006 expedition 1, 8, 14, 15–16, 114–24,
        127–34
    2008 expedition
        arrival in Pakistan 14–17, **15**
        ascent 1–8, **3**, **7**
        at Base Camp 45–8, **47**, **58**,
            58–63, 73–8, 86–7, 97–104, 114
        descent 11–13, 152–8, 164–9,
            167–8, **169**, **170**
        on the lower slopes: **59**, **60**, 61,
            73–7, 97–101, **102**, 125–7
        press reports 171–6
        puja ceremony **46**, 46–7, 59
        at the summit 8–11, **9–10**
        trek to Base Camp 24–8, **25**,
            26, **27**
    Base Camp 4, **27**, 28, 45–8, **47**, **58**, 58–

63, 73–8, 86–7, 97–104, 114, 158
Black Pyramid 44, **127**
Bottleneck 1, **3**, 3, 4–5, 6–7, 12, 45, 100–101, 155–7, 166, **172**, 173–5
Camp 1: 61, 74, 99
Camp 2: 4, 61, 73, 74–5, 76, 77, 87, 97–100
Camp 3: 4, 61, 73, 74, 75, 76, 87, 97–101, 125–7, 147
Camp 4: 5, 8, 12, 61, 76–7, 87, 97–101, 114, 147, 152, 155, 158
compared to Everest 2, 16
difficulty as climb 2, 16
fatality rate 2
Gilkey Memorial 97, **98**
history of climbs 44
House's Chimney 44
routes to summit **2**, 44–5, 73, **127**
summit 7, 8–11, **9–10**
Traverse 3, 4, **7**, 7–8, 11–12, 101, **153**, 156, 157, 175
views of **45, 75, 116**
weather 2, 4, 87, 97, 99, 101, 103–4, 114, 125–7
Karabelnikoff, Kenny **65**
Kashgar 109
Kathmandu 78, 91–3, 94, 95
Katmai National Park 64–6
Keenan, Mark 146
Khuburse torrent 26
Kiani, Major **161**
Kíla 141–3, 178
Kilcornan 2, 23, 28–30, 49, 71, 105–7, 142, 177–8
Kim Hyo-gyeong **188**
Kim Jae-soo 12, 77, 152, 155–6
King Mountain **184**, 185–6
Klinke, Chris 4, 6
Kodas, Michael 175
Korean team
climbing K2 5, 8, 12–13, 77–8, 103, 114
entangled climbers on descent 152–6, 158, 165–6, 168–9, 171, 174–7
Krantz, Randall 110–11
Kronthaler, Markus 123–4

Lama, Pasang 12, 174
Last Night's Fun 40, 64, **65**
Limerick 2, 23, 30, 107–8, 142, 181
Lynch, Donnacadha 38, **41**
Lynch, Sarah **41**

Lynch, Tracy **41**
McAleese, Mary 95, **108**, 108, 177
McDonnell, Denis 28, 35, 87, 88, 106
McDonnell, Denise 13, **32**, 33, 52, 107, 147–9, 159–64, 169, 175, **179, 182**
McDonnell, Fiona 181
McDonnell, Ger
in Alaska 17–23, 37–43, **39, 56**, 63–9, 108–9, 136, 138, 145, 146; *see also* Denali
in America 35–7, **36**
in Antarctica 135–7
asthma 25, 30, 118–19
Broad Peak climb **115, 117**, 117–23
childhood 28–33, **28–9, 31–2**
in China 109–11, **110**
at DCU 34–5
Denali
climbs 22–3, 48–57, **51**, 111–13, **112, 113**, 138–9
training for 17–22, 39, 43
dessert trolley prank 139–41
in England 33
Everest expedition (2003) 2, 15, 62, 72, 78–85, **80, 81**, 87–96
homecoming from **104**, 104–8, **106, 108**
plans for 63, 69–71
in Greece 33
head injury 8, 14, 129–34, 137, 142–3
K2 expedition (2006) 1, 8, 14, 15–16, 114–24, 127–34, **128**
K2 expedition (2008)
arrival in Pakistan 14–15, **15**
ascent 1, **1**, 3–5, 6–8
at Base Camp 45–8, **46, 47, 58**, 58–63, 73–8, 97–104, 114
descent 13, 152–6, 164–9, **167–8, 169, 170**
falls to death 156–7
on the lower slopes: **59, 60**, 61, 73–7, 97–101, **102**, 125–7
puja ceremony **46**, 46–7, 59
at the summit 8–11, **9–10**
training for 145–6
trek to Base Camp 25, **25, 26, 27**
loss of father 35
Marcus Baker climb 17–19, 20
memorials and tributes 177–89, **182, 184–5, 187, 188**

nieces and nephews **41**, 104, **137**, **187**, 187–9
press reports of death 171–6
in Scotland 69
and traditional music **39**, 39–42, 64, **65**, 141–3, 178, 181–2
McDonnell, Gertie 28, 30, **32**, 69, **104**, 104, 107, 138, 140, 148–9, 160–61, 178, **182**
McDonnell, J.J. 13, **31**, **32**, 32–3, 42–3, 64–9, 91–3, 107, 138, 140, 148, 149, 150–51, 160, 163, 169, 175, **182**
McDonnell, Martha 13, **32**, 33, 38, 107, 148–9, 161, **179**, **182**
McDonnell, Mary 139, 141
McDonnell, Mike 64, 65, 67, 68, 139–43
McDonnell, Stephanie **31**, **32**, 33, 40, 107, 147, 149, 161, **182**
McDonnell Peak **183**, 183–5
McDonough, Amber 185–6
McDonough, Jim 185, 186
Macken, Phelim 181
Mandić, Dren 6, 13, **188**
Marcus Baker 17–19, 20
Maryland 35, 37
Masherbrum 44, 46
Masherbrum Glacier 26
Mays, Mike 20–21, 22, 43, 48, 50–57
Meherban, Karim 8, **10**, 12–13, 44, 152, 156–7, 165–6, 171, 174, 179, **188**
Men's Journal 173, 174
Messner, Reinhold 16
Mexico 36
Meyer, Eric 4, 6, 78
Milford Hospice 22–3, 51, 53–4, 107
Mitre mountains 28
Morgan, Nora 143–5
Mount Foraker 69
Mount McKinley *see* Denali
Mount Tyree 71
Mulcair, John **31**, 32–3
Murphy, Mick
    Everest expedition (2003) 78, 82, 83–4, 88, 91, 92, 95
    Everest homecoming **108**
    K2 expedition (2006) 118, 120, 128–30, 133
Muztagh mountains 28

Nanga Parbat 24
Nash, John 161
Nash, Louisa 148

National Geographic Adventure 180
Naughton, David 108
Nessa, Lars 8, 11–12, 152
Neville, Dan 107, 108
Newcastle West 143
Nima (sherpa) 80, 82, 83
Norgay, Tenzing 14
North Carolina 37
Norway 35, 37
Norwegian team 5, 8, 11–12, 78
O'Brien, Damien 147–51, 161, 163, 175
O'Brien, Emma **41**, 161
O'Brien, Rebecca **41**, 104, 161, **187**, 187–9
O'Connell, Clare 150
O'Connell, Jerome 150
O'Connell, Micheál 138–9
O'Connor, David 149
O'Donoghue, Mike 161
O'Donovan, Derry 34
O'Keefe, Brian 187
O'Leary, Clare 72, 78, 90–91, 92, 95, 96, 105, **108**, **113**, 135, 136–7
O'Neill, Marie 135–6
O'Shaughnessy, Mike 29
Ó Snodaigh, Colm 141–3
Outside magazine 173, 175

Paiju Glacier 26
Paiju Peak 25
Park Kyeong-hyo **188**
Possumator, Dan **65**
Powers, Matt 174
Price, Kathryn 108
Prudhoe Bay 39, 63, 138

Quinn, Larry 180

Rakaposhi 24
Reid, Cliff 135
Reynolds, Tadhg **179**
Rice, Nick 45, 78, 154
Rigney, Ivan 177
Rinjee, Pemba 82, 83–4, 87–8, 91, 96
Roberts, Charles B. 22
Roche, John 113, **113**, 118
Rogg, Connie **184**, 185
Russian team 86

Scotland 69
Serbian team 6, 78, 86, 103
Shackleton, Ernest 135–6

Shannon Airport 138
Sheehan, Kevin 108
Sheen, Mark
    aftermath of Ger's death 163-4
    K2 expedition (2006) 15, 119, 120-22
    K2 expedition (2008) 2, **15**, 15-16, **25**,
        27, 61-2, 74-6, 99-101, 103
Shields, Hannah 72, 78, **81**, 82-3, 91, 92-3, 105
Shorten, George 78, **108**
Sjogren, Tina 176
Sjogren, Tom 176
Skardu 24, **25**, 76, 118-19, 130-32, 158
Skog, Cecilie 5, 8, 11, 78, 135, 152
Slattery, Liadain 69, 91-2, 141
South Georgia 135-7
South Pole expedition (planned) 137
Staleman, Jelle 14, **15**, **25**, **47**, 74-6, 97, 126,
        163, 164, 183-5
Stark, Rory 117
Starkey, Annie 8, 11, 13, 48, 109, **110**, 111,
        138, 148-9, 159, 162-4, 174-5, 178
Strang, Fredrik 4-5, 6

Talkeetna 49, 52, 69, 139
Teefy, Bridget 105, **106**, 106-7
Theos, Vernon 89
Thompson, Mike 19
Trango Towers 26, 46

Uli Biaho mountains 26
Urdukas 26

van de Gevel, Cas
    aftermath of Ger's death 152, 158, 162-
        3, 164-5, 173
    K2 expedition (2006) 14
    K2 expedition (2008) 5-11, 12, 14, **15**,
        25, **27**, 74-6, 97-8
van Eck, Maarten 8, 13, 24, 148, 149, 158
van Oss, Roeland 14, **25**, **27**, 74-6, 97, 99,
        100, 163, 165
van Rooijen, Wilco
    aftermath of Ger's death 147, 152-4,
        156, 158, 162-3, 166, 173, 175, 176
    K2 expedition (2006) 1, 14, 118, 119-21,
        122-3, 128-9, 133
    K2 expedition (2008) 1, **1**, 5-11, **10**, 12-
        13, 14, 24, **25**, **47**, 61, 74-6, 97
    Surviving K2 16
Viesturs, Ed 16, 180
Virginia 35, 37

Walsh, John 40, 42, 64, **65**
Waraich, Omar 174
Ward, Mark 64, **65**
Washburn, Barbara 49-50
Washburn, Brad 49-50
Waters, Ryan 128
Watson, David **172**
Whiting, Paul **182**
Wilkinson, Freddie, 171-5
Williams, Ben **110**
Willis, Grainne 92
Wixtead, Kathleen 107

Zerain, Alberto 4, 7